Master Your Philanthropy
How to maximize your strategic giving

Nicola Elkins

WINNIPEG, MANITOBA, CANADA

Nicola Elkins

MASTER YOUR PHILANTHROPY
How to maximize your strategic giving

©2009 Knowledge Bureau, Inc.

All rights reserved. No part of this publication may be reproduced, transmitted or otherwise used in any form or manner or stored in any data base or retrieval system without prior written permission of the publisher.

Much care has been taken to trace ownership of copyrighted material contained in this material, however, the publisher will welcome any information that enables it to rectify any reference or credit for subsequent editions.

The material in this publication is provided for informational purposes only. Laws, regulations, policy and procedures regarding this subject are continuously changing and the information and examples are intended as general guidelines only. This publication is sold with the understanding that the publisher is not engaged in rendering professional advice and it is recommended that such advice be obtained before acting on any of the information herein.

Readers of this book are responsible for their own actions and outcomes relating to this content and their personal finances and are advised to seek legal counsel or other professional advice before acting on any information or recommendations received. The owners, publishers, authors, and contributors expressly disclaim all and any liability to any person in respect of anything and any consequence as a result of the contents of this book. All names, scenarios and events noted in this book are fictious and any resemblance to real people and real situations is strictly coincidental.

ISBN 978-1-897526-30-9

Printed and bound in Canada

Library and Archives Canada Cataloguing in Publication

Elkins, Nicola, 1963-
    Master your philanthropy: how to maximize
your strategic giving / Nicola Elkins.

Includes bibliographical references and index.

    1. Charities—Canada. 2. Philanthropists—Charitable contributions—Canada. 3. Benefactors—Charitable contributions—Canada. I. Title.

HV41.9.C3E45 2009   361.7'40971   C2009-905199-0

Publisher:
Knowledge Bureau, Inc.
187 St. Mary's Road, Winnipeg, Manitoba Canada R2H 1J2
204-953-4769 Email: reception@knowledgebureau.com

Publisher and Managing Editor: Evelyn Jacks
General Manager: Norine Harty
Editorial Assistance: Brenda Griffith
Cover and Page Design: Sharon Jones

THE 10 Ps OF SUCCESSFUL WEALTH TRANSITION

Purpose
Ensure there is a purpose for the wealth so it can connect the family. Check that both generations have an understanding of the types of assets and why each is important to the transition.

Principles
Identify and share the beliefs and values that are important to uphold. This is the foundation for creating a "we focus."

Philosophy
Clarify what you want to achieve and the family legacy that you want to bestow. How should wealth be deployed going forward? This would include the vision for the future wealth protection and preservation, tax management, reinvestment or distribution, ongoing entrepreneurship, etc.

Participation
Engage all stakeholders in developing the purpose, principles and philosophy to get different viewpoints and find the common interest.

Philanthropy
Use this medium to test how stakeholders can work together and make financial decisions. See if you can create a sense of collective ownership among the next-generation beneficiaries.

Places to talk
Establish appropriate forums to enhance communication and build trust. Might include a family trust meeting, a wealth management advisory board and/or a family council.

Policies
Determine authority, responsibility and accountability around the future wealth distribution or reinvestment, individual compensation and financial independence and/or family ethics.

Plans
Create instructions for the implementation of the wealth transition and ongoing wealth management. Might include estate plans, continuity plan, family-participation plan, compensation plans and shareholder or other agreements.

Processes
Formalize the process to develop a wealth transition plan, groom heirs and nurture entrepreneurship. Begin with a strategy session. Might ultimately require a family office.

Passion
Use the above steps to develop the sincerity, sense of purpose, stewardship and trust that will guide the next-generation wealth managers.

— PT

love for their grandchildren and hope for their futures. At times there were tears, at times laughter as they recalled important events in their lives. Other than a few clarifying questions, I did not say much.

Requesting their story is a strategic step, as described in *Your Client's Story*, by Scott West and Mitch Anthony. They know their story up to this point in their lives; however, they don't know the future — where most advisers want to focus. Another important element of their story is the belief system that led to their success. These beliefs were summarized in such quotes as "we worked hard so our kids would have opportunities we didn't; we never smoked or drank; work was our vice; God blessed us; Canada is a great place for those who want to work hard."

When I asked why they hadn't moved forward on their estate freeze they could not really remember the tax memo, but when reminded the patriarch said, "Too much mumbo jumbo. My wife and I just want everything to go to my children and grandchildren and empathy, I first had to learn their story. Second, we had to communicate in terms the key stakeholders understood and could relate to; this did not include citing sections of the Income Tax Act. Third, we needed a process that communicated in simple terms the steps to take now and in the future.

The chart, above left, depicts the high-level steps we follow in our wealth transition process. Within each step are pictorial tools that have proven successful in communicating to our typically right-brained clients the steps we are taking and why.

Sense for clients and firms?

My experience over the past 10 years of integrating wealth advisory services with accounting firms is that a team is required to help affluent clients with their wealth management needs. If this team is coordinated to work in sync with a defined process it can deliver the best value to clients while developing a profitable wealth management division within an accounting firm. Since wealth management services are highly valued by clients and are typically provided on a fee as a percentage of client assets, the fees that accrue to this division generally provide greater profitability than traditional compliance services. Accounting firms need to ensure they are compliant with their provincial institute regulations, as it can be easy to cross the line — inadvertently.

Paul Tyers, CPA, CA, CFP, CIM, is managing director of Wealth Stewards Inc. He can be reached at ptyers@wealthstewards.ca or 1-866-515-5045

Key accomplishments in case study

Accomplishments	Team participants
Estate freeze completed	Accounting firm, valuator, law firm
Tax liability established at death and "funded" by life insurance	Accounting firm, insurance agent
Family business philosophy defined and who would be running the business	Business-transition adviser
Portfolio assets consolidated and managed	Portfolio manager, accounting firm (for ongoing tax minimization)

Acknowledgements

To the many people who have so generously shared their experiences with me and inspired me to find the field of gift planning fulfilling and important. Thank you for what you have given me and offered to others.

And to my family, Jonathan, Joely and Sabina, for their love and support.

Presents
Financial Education for Decision Makers

The Master Your Personal Finances Books:

Master Your Taxes
How to maximize your after-tax returns

Master Your Retirement
How to fulfill your dreams with peace of mind

Master Your Money Management
How to manage the advisors who work for you

Master Your Real Wealth
How to live your life with financial security

Master Your Philanthropy
How to maximize your strategic giving

Master Your Investment in the Family Business
How to increase after-tax wealth

Keep up your Mastery! For the latest in tax and personal financial planning strategies subscribe to Breaking Tax and Investment News. Visit www.knowledgebureau.com/masteryourtaxes

Knowledge Bureau Newsbooks are available at special discounts to use as sales promotions or for advisor/corporate training programs. For more information, address a query to
The Knowledge Bureau:
reception@knowledgebureau.com
1-866-953-4769
www.knowledgebureau.com

Contents

Introduction		7
Chapter 1	Understanding the Charitable Sector	11
Chapter 2	Gift Planning	19
Chapter 3	Develop Your Strategic Plan for Giving	37
Chapter 4	Selecting Your Cause	49
Chapter 5	Ways to Give	59
Chapter 6	Family Business and Philanthropy	69
Chapter 7	Grant Making and Foundation Management	79
Chapter 8	Monitor and Evaluate Your Impact	89
Chapter 9	Succession Planning for Your Philanthropy	99
Conclusion		111
Appendix		113
Index		117

Introduction

Canadians are becoming more philanthropic. We're giving more every year. But there is a major change in the way we are giving. We want to be more involved in making sure that our donations are doing as much good as they possibly can. And we want to develop powerful, cost-effective and tax-efficient strategies for our giving.

In today's world of heightened social awareness, the desire to make a difference is indeed gaining momentum, with people of all ages. More and more, individuals see their personal wealth not only as a means to live well, but also as a way to contribute to today's social needs or create a meaningful legacy for future generations. Whether your philanthropic vision is to support the arts, conserve natural resources, promote medical advances, or help an underprivileged child, giving back speaks volumes about who you are and the values you hold dear.

Master Your Philanthropy will help you to develop your strategic plan for philanthropy and learn about the many benefits of planned charitable giving. Not only will we explore some of the important trends in philanthropy today, but we'll show you how to develop your own plan for strategic philanthropy, and explain how you should take an investment approach to your charitable giving.

This is important, because evaluating a charity for a donation is just like evaluating a business for an investment. You should think about giving as though you are investing. You need to understand your cause, the charities that support it and the environment in which they operate. You also need to choose the specific charities you will support, have a long-term view, make sure you maximize any tax credits and benefits available to you, and monitor and evaluate your gift so that you can maximize the impact of your giving over time.

This book is also a useful resource for financial advisors who support clients inclined to give back. We will show you how to help clients make decisions with both purpose and process. That's important too, as the numbers grow significantly in the charitable donations sector and as we witness the aging of the powerful baby boom generation.

Boomers and their parents are driven by the desire to leave a legacy—through gifts of their time, knowledge, influence, cash and increasingly, in-kind by donating gifts of securities. Charitable donations in Canada topped $8.6 billion in 2007 for individual tax-filers—part of a growing trend to give back. Although the number of Canadians donating was down 1.6% over the previous year, those who give are giving more.

This upward trend in giving is due to a number of factors, besides the aging of the boomer demographic. Despite the recent market conditions, Canadians are increasingly wealthy. More households in Canada are considered high net worth (having investable assets of $1 million or more) than ever before. Awareness is on the rise, thanks to publicity from the likes of Bill Gates and Warren Buffet who are donating enormous wealth. Companies are partnering with charities on various fundraising initiatives as a way to give back while, at the same time, driving revenues. Canadians receive significant tax benefits, including a tax credit for the donation of securities to charities, and now without having to pay a capital gains tax on the appreciated value.

While the impact of the recent recession on donations for 2008 is not yet fully known, all indications are that over the long term this trend will continue as the country's baby boomers age. This is the generation that wanted to change the world. Now, as they retire, they have the time and the resources to make a difference. And there are a lot of them! Canada's

4.4 million pensioners already contribute nearly 30% of all charitable donations. They are the most generous donors and their number is expected to almost double by 2026. This is likely to spur a corresponding rise in donations, with high-net-worth individuals leading the way.

There is no doubt that Mastering Your Philanthropy is an issue of today and a powerful force in changing the world for a better tomorrow. This book will help you take part in this dynamic trend with vision, purpose and effectiveness.

THE FORMAT OF THIS BOOK

The principles for Mastering Your Philanthropy are discussed in this book in a straight-forward fashion, with common features to empower you. In each chapter you will find:

- *A True to Life Scenario:* These feature fictitious people in real-life situations supporting some exemplary Canadian charities and are a backdrop for the principles discussed in the chapter.
- *The Issues:* What is important and why?
- *The Solutions:* What do you need to know and do to make the right decisions for your philanthropy? How can you best integrate these solutions in your overall wealth-management plan to meet goals by asking the right questions?
- *A Success Story:* Most chapters feature an interview with a real-life philanthropist or gift planning expert.
- *The Mastery:* Tips and Traps to help you put your charitable decision making into focus, simplify your efforts, and get better results.

We trust you'll find this format useful in taking control and making better charitable decisions either on your own, or together with your team of financial advisors.

NICOLA ELKINS AND
THE KNOWLEDGE BUREAU

CHAPTER 1

Understanding the Charitable Sector

We make a living by what we get, but we make a life by what we give.
WINSTON CHURCHILL

> Karen just inherited a windfall. Her father died and left a substantial sum to her in his will. His death and the inheritance was a major event that caused her to reflect on her own life. Karen and her husband were teachers who had recently retired, their children were grown, they had their health. Life was good. The time has come for them to start giving back.
>
> Karen realized that while she had been teaching young children to read for her entire career, 1 in 6 adult Canadians struggle to read the headlines of a newspaper. She had heard about Frontier College, a national literacy organization that provides vital literacy programs to children and adults. This was a potential partner that could help her give both her time, to help people learn to read through her local literacy program, and her money to support this important cause.
>
> Karen wanted to donate a substantial sum, but before she committed to her charity she still had many questions to answer: How much are other Canadians donating and where are those dollars going? Which charities are dealing with the problems important to me? Do they have sufficient funding and where do they get their funding from? How do I make a donation most effectively? Who can help me?

THE ISSUES

How do you choose the right charity to steward your money towards the cause you are passionate about and spend the resources you will allocate to it, wisely? It's an important question and an issue on the minds of many new philanthropists. The first step to mastering your own philanthropy is to understand the landscape in which you are operating.

Like all good teachers, Karen decided to do her homework first. She contacted her financial advisor to help her understand how much she could give and how to do so in a manner that met her goals. She, in the meantime, would do her research on charities involved in literacy in Canada.

The Charitable Sector is Growing

The charitable sector in Canada is large and it is growing. There are over 161,000 not-for-profit and volunteer organizations. About half have charitable registration status from Canada Revenue Agency; that number has been growing consistently for many years. The sector includes "day-care centres, sports clubs, arts organizations, social clubs, private schools, hospitals, food banks, environmental groups, trade associations, places of worship, advocates for social justice, and groups that raise funds to cure diseases". The charitable sector reports a combined volunteer complement of over 19 million, and over 2 million paid staff[1].

Funding Sources and Recipients are Changing

Revenue flow to charities is growing consistently at a rate of 7.6% a year—reaching over $174 billion in 2007. And total revenues are expected to grow to over $200 billion dollars annually by 2012[2]. If you look at the sector in terms of Canada's managed money market, it is a significant player. Its estimated size in December of 2007 was $210 billion, or an 8% share of the entire managed money market in Canada[3].

---

[1] National Survey of Not-For-Profit and Voluntary Organizations. Statistics Canada. Revised Edition 2005.
[2] Compound Annual Growth Rate CAGR

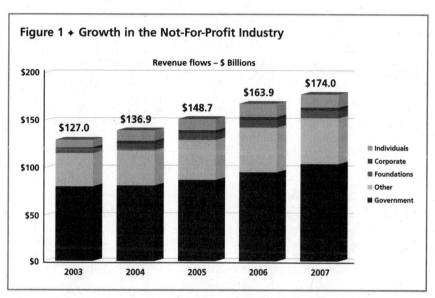

Source: Statistics Canada, Investor Economics. *Corporate data estimated.

While the growth described above is expected to continue, the sources of funding are changing. The government is still the largest contributor by far, although recent years have seen significant and continuing cutbacks. Charities are increasingly generating revenue by other means. Earned income (fees and other revenues generated by the charities themselves and included in *Other* in Figure 1) is the next biggest revenue generator, followed by individual taxpayers, foundations and corporations in that order.

In recent years, donor priorities have been shifting. In 2006, social agencies represented 19% of the total, compared to health care organizations which represented 39%. In 2008 corresponding figures were 26% for social agencies and 32% for health care[4]. The new realities of recent economic circumstances appear to be raising the priority of social agencies to the detriment of health and education organizations.

---

[3]Figure 1 – Investor Economics: 2009 Charitable Giving
[4]Investor Economics: 2009 Charitable Giving

Charity Legislation is Changing

Despite the broad range of charitable organizations across the country, charities are alike in a number of ways. Charitable registration status allows them to be exempt from a variety of taxes and enables their donors to claim tax credits for donations. These organizations are also alike in their pursuit to serve the public, as well as their legal structure which does not allow the profits to be distributed to owners or directors.

Tax Law is Changing Too

But perhaps the most significant event in recent years happened in 2006 when the government announced changes to the tax rules governing donations. These changes provided incentives to taxpayers by eliminating capital gains on donation of securities that are publicly traded. When shares are sold, the securities are subject to taxation. The new tax law virtually eliminates the capital gains tax on listed securities if they are donated directly to a registered charity. As a result, it is more beneficial for the donor to donate a security directly to the charity, than for the donor to sell the security and donate the proceeds in cash.

THE SOLUTIONS

To Master Your Philanthropy it is clear that you can be more effective with a team approach. Consider working with a professional financial advisor, like Karen did. More and more, people are turning to their financial advisors for help in this area. Advisors—including legal, accounting and financial advisors—all have an important role in helping their clients make their charitable decisions. Increasingly, people are using consultants to help them evaluate the charities they select. Canadians are becoming far more demanding in wanting to maximize the impact of their gifts and are holding charities accountable to show them how they have done so.

If you have millions of dollars to donate, then you might consider establishing your own private foundation. But if your resources are smaller, and/or if you are not comfortable with the level of administration and corporate procedure that goes along with your own foundation, there are other options. Recent years have witnessed the growth of community foundations and other national public charitable foundations whose primary job is to connect investors and their advisors with worthy charities through the creation of donor advised funds and endowments.

Today, many financial service organizations are focusing on providing new innovative products like donor-advised funds. They are helping their advisors to assist clients in integrating charitable giving into their financial planning. Use your advisors as a resource to help you to maximize your strategic giving, while minimizing your tax burdens.

IN SUMMARY

Who is a philanthropist? Is it you and me or one of the world's few ultra-rich? It can, in fact, be each of us. Our first success story explains how to be one effectively.

SUCCESS STORY

Diane MacDonald, the Executive Director of the Canadian Association of Gift Planners, explains from her vantage point. "Gift planning is the donor-centered process that meets philanthropic goals now and in the future, while balancing personal, family, and tax considerations. Our organization encourages collaboration among various stakeholders to ensure that the gift planning process achieves a fair and proper balance between the interests of donors and the aims and objectives of registered charitable organizations in Canada."

The professional advisor members work with wealthy people to help them achieve their charitable goals. "Advisors help donors to understand that being a philanthropist isn't just about writing a cheque. Many donors start out by getting involved in an issue that they are passionate about. They often have a long-term commitment to their cause and consistently engage others in their charities of choice."

As Diane says, "Success…is when a donor has a cause that is dear to their heart and is able to achieve the most effective giving strategy to support that cause by working with a collaborative team of advisors. This is what we call 'inspired giving through enlightened and informed planning.'"

THINGS YOU NEED TO KNOW

- The charitable sector is large and growing.
- Traditional trends of funding sources and recipients are changing.
- Legislation and tax incentives are favourable for giving in Canada.
- Advisors are playing an increasing role in helping clients with philanthropy.

QUESTIONS YOU NEED TO ASK

- Why are you interested in giving back?
- What are the things you care about most?
- What is the problem you want to address?

THINGS YOU NEED TO DO

- Your homework! Research is important so that you can understand the issues surrounding your cause and answer these important questions. Only then can you develop your own strategic plan for giving.

DECISIONS YOU NEED TO MAKE

- Choose your cause.
- Resolve how you are going to get involved. Time? Money?
- Determine what to give and how to give it.

MASTER YOUR PHILANTHROPY
Understanding the Charitable Sector

TIPS

- Mastering your philanthropy begins with finding your passion, doing your homework and creating a plan to achieve permanent change.
- Find an advisor you can discuss your goals with.
- Understand your cause and the environment charities in that area operate in.
- Get involved.
- Resolve to direct your donations.

TRAPS

- Chequebook philanthropy doesn't ensure your gift will have an impact.
- Make sure you consult your advisor to ensure you get the most effective gift planning solution for your gifts.

Principle Mastery: If you are going to give, give wisely. Having a strategic gift plan helps you to meet your philanthropic goals now and in the future, while balancing personal, family, and tax considerations.

CHAPTER 2

Gift Planning

...it is prodigious the quantity of good that may be done by one man if he will make a business of it. BENJAMIN FRANKLIN

> Christina and her best friend Beth have been together since grade school, sharing all of life's ups and downs. But Beth was diagnosed with early onset Alzheimer's disease a few years back and she passed away this year. It has been a devastating process for Beth's family and everyone involved but Christina is optimistic that today's researchers are close to a cure for Alzheimer's.
>
> Christina wants to give something back in memory of her friend. By giving to research through the Toronto General & Western Hospital Foundation, she can help in the fight to prevent the onset of this debilitating illness. Dr. Peter St. George-Hyslop, an internationally acclaimed geneticist and physician, and his team of researchers have identified a key protein involved in the degeneration of nerve cells in Alzheimer's disease.
>
> Christina is now 55, unmarried and still very active and involved in her job. She has done well working for her employer, but has little time for herself these days as she has recently been promoted. Over the past 25 years she has built up a considerable investment portfolio,

plus she has stock options in the company. But Christina isn't sure how to go about giving her gift. She has heard that there are some tax advantages to making donations and she wants to be smart about how she gives her money away. She certainly doesn't want to give any more to the tax man than she has to. Who can help her to execute her plan?

THE ISSUES

Gift planning is the process of designing charitable gifts so that the donor realizes their philanthropic objectives while maximizing tax and other financial benefits. It is about determining what to give, and when and how to give it. An experienced gift planner is just what Christina is looking for, but the reality today is that the majority of estate planners and financial advisors do not talk with their clients about their charitable objectives. Many advisors are concerned that clients will consider this kind of questioning too personal or a judgment on them if they don't give, and many are also concerned that they don't have the right level of expertise to raise the topic. Fortunately, in Canada there are a growing number of advisors involved in philanthropy and there are many innovative solutions that the Government has put in place to assist with tax-advantaged giving. Christina has made a good start by deciding to seek the help of her advisors before making her charitable donation decisions.

For Christina, planning her gift really boils down to these four things:

- Reviewing her resources,
- Understanding charitable gifts and their tax aspects,
- Deciding whether to give now or give later, or both,
- Determining the most tax-efficient solution for her circumstances.

Perhaps some of these solutions will ring true for you, too.

THE SOLUTIONS

Reviewing Your Resources

The first thing you need to determine is "Do you have enough?" How much you give depends on how much you have, how much you will likely spend before you pass away, and how much you want to leave to your heirs. You want to ensure you are:

- Maximizing your wealth,
- Minimizing your liabilities (especially taxes),
- Providing for your heirs,
- Providing a contingency for unexpected changes in your circumstances,
- Still ensuring that your chosen cause has the ability to continue its work.

To do this, you need to integrate your charitable planning into your overall estate and/or business succession plan.

There are many considerations to take into account in tax and estate planning, and you should consult with your advisors, as Christina chose to do. It is always a good idea to keep your will up to date at all times with a complete list of beneficiaries, both primary and secondary, and you should have appropriate power of attorney and medical power of attorney (or health care directive) documents in place. Remember to ensure that your registered retirement savings plans and life policies continue to reflect your current list of beneficiaries. Incomplete or inconsistent documentation for your estate can lead to delays and objections.

You should be sure to make a list of your assets (investments, real estate, etc.) and your liabilities to determine the value of your estate; liabilities will have to be paid before your estate can distribute the assets as you have instructed. You will need to choose an executor to carry out your instructions on your behalf. Most importantly, your legal and financial advisors will be able to help you with tax planning and property transfer strategies to help to maximize your estate and minimize your taxes, and they can also assist you with planning your charitable gifts—both gifts you may wish to give now and those you wish to defer until you pass away. The goal is to meet your philanthropic goals now and in the future, while balancing personal, family and tax considerations.

Once you have determined the size of your gifts, you will be better able to determine exactly how you want to intervene to maximize your social impact. Remember, you don't have to be a millionaire to be a philanthropist. Even small resources can tackle large problems when pooled with others. Middle class Canadians are among the most generous donors, particularly once their children have grown and/or they enter retirement. Many find themselves with more disposable income and more time to support their favourite causes.

Whether your gift is large or small, you will need to decide on the scope of the impact you are trying to achieve. Do you want to give at home or internationally? Do you want to make a short-term impact that you can measure quickly, or are you tackling a long-term, life threatening and complex problem? The latter implies far more risk, but potentially a much greater reward, although it may take years to achieve.

Consider setting aside a specific amount each year for unplanned giving. Although you will be focused on your cause, you may want to be able to respond to a specific request or an event that puts people at risk. Ultimately, where you decide to intervene depends on where you think you can make the greatest impact given your financial and other resources (for example, helping the needy vs. preventing the problem from recurring).[1] The important thing is to strike the right balance between your financial, personal and charitable objectives.

Charitable Gifts and Taxes

Tax credits reduce your tax payable. Tax deductions reduce your taxable income. How your tax options co-mingle to help you get the results you want for your benefactors is important. Here's a brief basic primer of tax preferences available to you.

---

[1] Brest, Paul and Harvey, Hal. *Money Well Spent: A Strategic Plan for Smart Philanthropy*. 2008.

For individuals, donation receipts for the amounts you give to your favourite registered charity allow you to claim a tax credit on your return. If you donate over $200, you can receive a tax credit at your highest combined federal and provincial marginal rate. However, there is an annual donation limit. Your tax credit in any given year cannot exceed 75% of your net income. That includes income from all sources, including employment, pension, interest, dividends and capital gains, less some deductions (like RRSP contributions). The good news is that any excess can be carried forward for the next 5 years. For your estate, this limit is increased to 100% of net income in the year of your death and any excess can be carried back to the year prior.

For companies, donations are treated as a deduction that is based on the type of income earned. The deductions are particularly tax advantageous for corporations with specified investment business income derived from property including interest, dividends, rents and royalties. The same carry forward rules and 75% limits apply. So, if you are a business owner, it may be more advantageous for you to give through the company than personally.

Giving Now or Giving Later

Another consideration in planning your gifts is "Do you want to give now or later, or both?" There are many ways other than donating cash that allow you to give during your lifetime, including gifting securities, life insurance policies, gift annuities and more. And there are many ways to give after you have passed on, including leaving a bequest in your will, donating registered plan assets or life insurance policy proceeds by making a charity the beneficiary. Let's look at some of these now.

Giving Now

Cash gifts are one of the simplest ways to give—you will receive a tax receipt for the amount donated. The receipt provides a tax credit to reduce the total tax payable in the year you make the donation, as discussed previously.

Capital Property gifts include real estate, art, etc. A tax receipt is issued for the fair market value of the gift and 50% of the gain is taxable.

Certified Cultural Property may be claimed by donors who own property that has been determined to be of outstanding significance and national importance may receive a tax certificate for the fair value of the property by the Canadian Cultural Property Export Review Board. No gain will be taxable to the donor upon the donation. Like cultural property, *Ecologically-Sensitive Land* or 'Eco-Gifts' may be donated through the Ecological Gifts Program, which must register the property. Normally, these agreements allow the donor to continue to own the land, live on it and pass it to heirs.

Publicly Traded Securities that have appreciated over time are an effective way to maximize charitable giving, while minimizing tax burdens. Not only will you receive a tax receipt for the fair market value of securities on the day of donation but you will also pay no tax on the capital gains, provided the gift is a qualifying security (listed on a public exchange), bond or a mutual fund. Giving appreciated public securities is better than selling them and giving the cash proceeds, but it is important to note that to receive this additional tax benefit you must donate the stock; don't sell and transfer cash, because this will trigger a capital gains tax liability.

Employee Stock Options provide employees with a right to buy shares in their employer's company at a future date for a set price. If you have stock options with an exercise price below the fair market value, you can buy the shares at a lower price and immediately sell them on the open market for a profit. On the sale, a taxable benefit is incurred for the difference between the fair market value when the security was acquired and the exercise price. However, if you donate the proceeds within 30 days of the exercise, the donation is treated as if it were a publicly traded security, so you will pay no capital gains tax on the portion you donate to charity. This will be an excellent opportunity for Christina to consider in reviewing her gift plan.

Gift-Matching Programs are offered by many employers as part of employee benefits. If you work for a company with a gift-matching program, you can take advantage and double or even triple your gift depending on the company's policy. It is an easy way to give, because your employer processes everything and you don't have to write a cheque every pay period.

Charity Events are another great way to get involved and have some fun! These events go beyond the more traditional gala dinners to challenge events like walks, runs, or bike rides. You can donate your time as a volunteer, participate in the event and seek sponsorship from your friends and colleagues, or you can pay to attend the event and bid for auctioned items. You will get a tax receipt for the difference between the fair market value cost of the actual event or item and the revenue from the ticket sales or bid. In other words, the eligible amount of the gift for your tax receipt is based on the donation less the cost of any 'advantage' to you.

Endowments empower donors who want to give larger gifts for specific causes. An endowment is a fund from which only the income is allocated for charitable purposes, leaving the original donation intact. Once established, you can add to an endowment fund at any time, and only you can change the rules or make decisions about the distribution of income. Endowment fund gifts receive a tax receipt in the year of donation. They are a great way to create a legacy that allows you (or others) to donate now, with the knowledge that your contribution will continue in perpetuity.

Donor-Advised Funds are charitable giving vehicles created for the purpose of managing charitable donations and are, like an endowment, tailored to reflect your family's philanthropic goals and values. When the fund is established you can name the fund and select the charitable organization or causes that the fund will support. You can often advise the charity on how you would like the income from your fund to be used each year. You will also receive an immediate tax receipt on your donations. The charitable organization handles all the administrative details and should provide you with regular reporting. Donor Advised Funds are a flexible and cost-effective method of leaving a lasting legacy—similar to establishing your own foundation, but without the time and expense required to manage one. This is another effective route for Christina to consider as she wants control over where her grants will go, but has little time to administer her gifts.

Gifts of Insurance can be made either during your lifetime or deferred until after you have gone. To donate now, you could transfer the ownership of an existing paid-up life insurance policy to your charity or purchase a new policy and transfer ownership. Either way, the charity should assign itself as the beneficiary. For existing policies, your insurance company can help you to assess the fair market value of the policy in order to determine your donation tax receipt amount. For new policies you will receive tax receipts annually for payment of the premiums.

Giving Later

For many people, giving during their lifetime is a gratifying experience that allows them to be involved in a cause close to their heart. However, not everyone is in a position to make that financial decision during their lifetime and still protect the balance between their financial, personal and charitable objectives. If this sounds like you, your strategy for giving may involve a deferred gift. There are several options for deferred gifts that offer tax benefits and preservation of economic security for you and your loved ones.

Bequests are charitable gifts left in your will. They represent an easy and powerful way to ensure continued support for the causes that you care about, and demonstrate your commitment to an ongoing legacy of philanthropy. As the first substantial charitable gift you ever make, or as part of a long history of giving, charitable bequests signal an unwavering commitment to your values and to the kind of world you envision for future generations. You should use a lawyer to advise you when making your will and it is a good idea to contact your charity if you plan to make a bequest. Their legal department can often help to guide you and your lawyer to make sure that your will clearly sets out how your estate should deal with your charitable wishes. If possible, it is a good idea to tell your other beneficiaries about your wishes in advance. This will help to avoid confusion and/or objections after you are gone.

Gifts of RRSPs and RRIFs can support your charitable interests, while realizing significant tax advantages for your estate. They are most appropriate on the death of the second spouse. The remaining proceeds of RRSPs and/or RRIFs are taxable in the final tax return. Naming a charity as your RRSP or RRIF beneficiary can offset a substantial portion of the tax owed by your estate. The amount creditable on your final tax return is 100% of income, not 75%. Plus, you can carry-back any excess tax credit one year. To make sure your estate can manage this effectively, it is a good idea to ensure the plan documents and your will have signed documents specifying the correct beneficiaries.

Gifts of Life Insurance can also be used as a charitable asset, enabling you to make a substantial gift in the future. If you want to use life insurance to relieve taxes on your estate, then you could consider donating your life insurance proceeds through your will. Insurance death benefits are non-taxable, which means your estate can receive a large tax-free lump sum to pay your taxes or give to charity. You won't be eligible for a tax receipt now, but your estate can claim up to a maximum of 100% of your income in the year you die and the year prior.

Some Techniques for Tax-Efficient Gift Planning

Gifts of Flow-Through Limited Partnerships

If you are a charitably inclined investor, sensitive to tax and have the stomach for high risk investments, you could consider gifting shares of a Flow-Through Limited Partnership. Another way that the government is encouraging donations, as well as investment in small resource companies, is through investors who buy units of Limited Partnerships (LP) that invest in shares of those resource companies. The company renounces its development costs; the investors use these expenses as a deduction in income and over two to three years completely write off the cost of the shares. The LP then converts its holdings into a mutual fund; as the shares are now publicly traded securities they can be donated, with the investor receiving a fair-market-value tax receipt. The capital gain on the securities can be significant, so these 'flow-through shares' can considerably improve the tax efficiency of charitable donations. They are, however, highly speculative investments and therefore high risk.

Ultimately, the investor can win three ways:

- Writing off the capital cost of the securities against income.
- Reducing the capital cost of the units to zero and realize a capital gain, which is taxed more favourably than income.

- If the securities are owned by a personal corporation, the entire gain can be placed into the Capital Dividend Accounts (CDA) to be paid out to shareholders on a tax-free basis.[2]

Insured Share Bequest for the Private Business Owner

If you are a charitably inclined business owner with a holding company, insurable, over aged 60 and worth upwards of $1,000,000, you might consider an Insured Share Bequest. This would allow you to donate shares of your private company when you pass on. Let's assume you freeze $2,000,000 worth of your company shares today at fair market value. Your holding company takes out a joint life insurance policy on you and your spouse for half that; it will pay no tax on the proceeds. Yes, there will be insurance costs and you will have to amend your will to bequest, let's say, half the frozen shares, worth $1,000,000, to your favourite charity; but on the death of the second spouse your estate will get a tax credit to use to pay other taxes. Plus, the life insurance company will pay the insurance proceeds to your holding company tax-free and it can put the money into the Capital Dividend Account. The holding company can then use these proceeds to buy back the shares bequeathed to the charity and it can repurchase the remaining shares from the estate via a promissory note (the shareholders can get a $1,000,000 IOU from the holding company). Because the money was in the Capital Dividend Account, it can be paid out tax free at any time to the shareholders.

The net result is a significant donation to your favourite cause, an increased value to your heirs/shareholders and significantly decreased estate taxes.[3]

Wealth Replacement—Registered Plan and Insurance

If you have an RRSP or a RRIF and you are concerned about estate taxes, naming the charity as the beneficiary for RRSP or RRIF usually eliminates the tax on this investment. On your death, your estate will pay up to 50% in tax before the assets are transferred to your heirs. By insuring the registered plan, you can provide the funds to pay the tax

---

[2] Osborne, DeWayne. *A Charitable Guide to Gift Planning.* Lawton Partners, 2009.
[3] Cestnick, Tim. *Social Capital and Social Entrepreneurship.* Waterstreet/CAGP, 2009.

without depleting the value of the inheritance for your heirs, because they will receive tax-free insurance proceeds on your death.

For example, let's say you have a RRIF valued at $250,000. On your death, you'll pay $100,000 in taxes and the estate will get $150,000. If, on the other hand, you purchased a life insurance policy and bequeath the RRIF to charity, your estate will get a $250,000 donation receipt, which provides a tax credit (assuming 40%) worth $100,000, eliminating your tax bill. Premiums will have to be paid, but you can leave more to your heirs and your favourite charity too.

Charitable Life Annuity Strategy

If you are a charitably inclined donor aged 70 with a portfolio of GICs, and you like the idea of protecting your cash, you might consider a charitable gift plus a life annuity strategy. Let's say you transfer GICs worth $100,000 in exchange for a tax deduction. The funds are separated into two payments: one for an immediate gift to charity of $25,000 and the remaining funds to purchase an annuity from an insurance company. The details of the annuity are based on your age and the purchase amount. You receive an immediate tax receipt for the $25,000 gift and the annuity payments are guaranteed for life.

Donating Optioned Stock Cash Proceeds

If you, like Christina, hold stock options, an advisor can explain the advantages in terms of donating optioned stock proceeds. The Income Tax Act allows a cash donation, funded by an exercised option, to be treated as if it were a publicly traded security. Christina will receive a tax receipt for her donation and, provided the donation is made within 30 days of the exercise, the portion donated is not subject to capital gains tax. She owns 10,000 employee stock options coming due. Her options are worth $50 per share and the exercise price is $20. Her marginal tax rate is 45%. She wishes to donate 20% of her proceeds or $100,000 to research. She instructs the broker to sell all 10,000 units. The table below shows the difference between total proceeds if no gift is provided, vs. Christina's 20% gift.

Donating Optioned Stock Cash Proceeds	No Gift	Gift	
		Keep	Donated
Cash from sale	$500,000	$400,000	$100,000
Exercise price (Adjusted Cost Base/Fair Market Value)	$200,000	$160,000	$40,000
Gain on sale	$300,000	$240,000	$0
Tax on gain (gain x 50% x Marginal Tax Rate)	$67,500	$54,000	$0
Tax savings (gift x 45%)	n/a	n/a	$45,000
Total proceeds (cash – exercise price – tax)	$232,000	$231,000	

For virtually the same total proceeds, Christina has donated $100,000 to a donor advised fund named after her beloved Beth, with the grants going to Alzheimer's research.

IN SUMMARY

Like Christina, you may be looking for help in determining a good way to give that will also be smart and tax-efficient. As a first step, look for a qualified advisor who understands the process of gift planning. You can design charitable gifts so that you realize your philanthropic objectives while maximizing tax and other financial benefits. If you are an advisor looking to understand the gift planning process better, investigate the Canadian Association of Gift Planners. The CAGP have some valuable educational seminars and courses for you to consider.

Now, please consider a success story from the 'street'. Advisors in particular will be interested in this success story from an experienced gift planner.

SUCCESS STORY

Keith Thomson is a founder and Managing Director of Stonegate Private Counsel LP, which specializes in handling the affairs of high-net-worth families. Keith holds the Certified Financial Planner (CFP®) designation and is a member of the Canadian Association of Gift Planners. Acting upon his strong beliefs in the importance of giving back to his community, Keith has been a director of the Toronto Community Foundation and is the current Chair of the African Medical and Research Foundation in Canada. Here is what Keith had to say about gift planning in Canada:

"The challenge today is that many advisors don't incorporate it into their financial planning process or even talk to their clients about it, either because they think it is too personal or because they don't have in-depth knowledge of the subject. That is certainly how I felt when I started, but I don't anymore. For clients who are charitably inclined it is absolutely a key part of their overall wealth management plan, not to mention a great way to solidify your relationship with a client. And even for clients who are not, I believe that it is our fiduciary responsibility as advisors to make them aware of the solutions available to them.

"The advisor's first priority is to be crystal clear about how much their clients have and whether it is enough to fund their lifestyle for the rest of their lives; then discuss how much they wish to leave their heirs. Once that is determined we can start to talk about what they want to leave behind for charity. One technique I use if clients are inclined to charitable giving is our Thanksgiving matching program. We provide a match of up to $250.00 to our clients' favourite charity. It is an easy entry to have a bigger conversation about philanthropy and it allows me to connect with my clients on a values basis, which is by far the most important conversation to have—understanding what is important to them.

"For those who are less inclined to give, I take another approach. It isn't a judgment about whether they give or not, it just makes sense from a tax perspective for people who want to minimize the tax they pay. The truth is that most people are not aware that the government has created effective rules and laws because they want us to give. They have provided us with a massive tool box to convert assets in a tax-advantaged way into gifts. I ask clients if they realize that, on their passing, they can allocate what would have gone to the CRA to a cause that is important to them. I then explain how they have a choice; they can either give involuntarily through taxes and allow the government to choose where those dollars go, or they can give voluntarily through gift planning and have some control over the direction of their gifts. That usually gets people listening.

"Charity brings meaning to our lives. Once we reach a certain age, we tend to reflect on the things that are most important to us—and it isn't usually how much time you've spent at the office, but family, people and causes that are important to us. Gift planning helps people find a way to actualize their values and to pass them on to their children and grandchildren down the road."

THINGS YOU NEED TO KNOW

- Your gift planning goal is to meet your philanthropic goals now and in the future, while balancing personal, family, and tax considerations.
- There is an annual donation limit. Your tax credit in any given year cannot exceed 75% of your net income, except in the year of death.
- There are many ways to give tax-efficiently, and both cash or certain properties may be donated. You may be familiar with giving cash to registered charities. However, donating certain securities may provide significant tax benefits.
- Other options include gifting through Donor Advised Funds, which are a flexible and cost-effective method of leaving a lasting legacy—similar to establishing your own foundation—but without the time and expense required to manage one.
- There are many ways to give insurance:
  1. Donate an existing policy.
  2. Purchase a new policy and transfer ownership.
  3. Donate the proceeds of a policy through your will and estate.
  4. Use an insurance policy to replace the wealth of a donated RRIF.
  5. Gifts plus annuities

QUESTIONS YOU NEED TO ASK

- Ask your financial advisors to help you with your plans for charitable giving to ensure tax planning and property transfer strategies are put in place.
- If you are an employee with stock options, ask your advisor about the tax benefits of donating a portion of the stock.

THINGS YOU NEED TO DO

- Integrate your charitable gift planning into your overall estate and/or business succession plan.
- Keep your will up to date at all times along with appropriate power of attorney and medical power of attorney documents.
- Ensure that your registered retirement savings plans and life policies continue to reflect your current list of beneficiaries.

DECISIONS YOU NEED TO MAKE

- Do you want to give now, later, or both? The vehicles you chose for giving will depend on the timing of your gift.

MASTER YOUR PHILANTHROPY
Gift Planning

TIPS

- Giving appreciated public securities is better than selling them and giving the cash proceeds, because you will receive a tax receipt for the fair market value of securities on the day of donation, which you can use for a tax credit AND you will pay no tax on the capital gains.

TRAPS

- If you are gifting securities, make sure your broker doesn't sell them before transferring the funds to your charity. This will trigger the capital gain. You must donate securities in-kind by transferring the shares to your charity's account.

Principle Mastery: Avoid giving involuntarily through your tax dollars. Make sure your gifts work to your advantage and use the tax benefits available to you to maximize your gifts and the social return on your investments.

CHAPTER 3

Develop Your Strategic Plan for Giving

To give away money is an easy matter and in any man's power. But to decide to whom to give it and how large and when, and for what purpose and how, is neither in every man's power nor an easy matter. ARISTOTLE

> *James sits as a Chairman of the Board on his grandfather's private foundation. He has enjoyed a wonderful legacy of philanthropy and his family has taught him the value of giving back to his community. But James has a problem. His grandfather was passionate about funding medical research. James lives in the city and he is passionate about the urban environment. His favourite cause is Evergreen, Canada's leading urban-based environmental non-profit organization that has a mandate to bring green space back to urban areas through widespread restoration and conservation programs.*
>
> *The objectives of the private foundation are narrow and constrain the foundation's granting capability from branching out into new and exciting areas of scientific research. He is sure that his grandfather would approve of his suggestions, but he and the Board can't implement them without significant cost to the foundation to change its charter and adjust its objectives. How could James' family have avoided this unfortunate circumstance?*

THE ISSUES

How do you ensure your values are reflected in your philanthropy and that your loved ones are aligned in dealing with your chosen cause? Every great plan identifies what success is and how to get there, but what is success for your family philanthropy? How is it managed through a successful start and to a successful conclusion? How do you instill a culture of proactive commitment to family and community on an ongoing basis? If you are successful in doing so during your lifetime, how do you pass along the strategic direction, policies and procedures for investing that you have developed after you are gone? What are the consequences of a directionless effort?

Giving effectively—and sustainably—requires that you make a plan and then stick to it with informed choices. There is no right or wrong here. What is important is what matters to you. However, your vision for strategic giving is more likely to succeed if you have a defined process in place starting with a strategic direction or mission statement and some specific objectives that govern both your giving and action plans coming out of your donation.

Even if you have a vision or mission statement in place, many families like James' find that not everyone agrees on philanthropy as individuals or as a part of a family. That can be problematic right from the start, and continue long after the philanthropist passes away.

THE SOLUTIONS

Setting a strategic direction for family giving involves an internal review of your values and personal experience and a focus on the causes you care about. In doing your research, it is important that you identify and involve your key stakeholders. As with any other formal planning, you should document the first part of your strategic plan.

What principles will govern your strategic decision making? Are your family values aligned with the individual stakeholders? Is your charity aligned with your family values? What rules will you rely on to provide direction when things change—time, resources, governance?

How to Develop a Strategic Plan

The components of a successful strategic plan include the following:

- Setting your strategic direction
- Aligning family values
- Documenting your strategy
- Setting achievable objectives

Setting Your Strategic Direction

Your family mission statement around philanthropic giving should be succinct and stand the test of time. To develop it, UK Philanthropy, a leading resource for impartial advice to aspiring philanthropists who want to give effectively, has provided guidance in the form of three Key Principles in this area[1].

- **Give responsibly.** Be knowledgeable about the causes and organizations you are supporting. Even if you do not have time to engage directly with the recipients of your gifts, read the evaluation reports and modify your plans as appropriate.
- **Understand the impact of your giving.** Be confident that you are achieving your objectives. What impact do you seek? What impact do you have on the organization and on its beneficiaries?
- **Seek advice.** There are a variety of good and experienced sources who can advise you on your giving plan and on individual gift investments. These include professional advisory services as well as informal sources of support such as family, friends and colleagues.

A good example of a succinct mission with longevity can be found at the J.W. McConnell Family Foundation. It describes its vision as being "to fund projects in Canada that foster citizen engagement, build resilient communities and have the potential for national scale or impact" and its mission is "to support Canadians in building a society that is inclusive, sustainable and resilient".

---

[1] *Philanthropy UK: A Guide to Giving.* 3rd edition.

The vision/mission acknowledges that the foundation will give responsibly by funding projects with the potential for national scale or impact, and that it understands the impact of its gifts as being effective in fostering citizen engagement. The foundation's website outlines how it seeks advice on an ongoing basis to ensure it remains a learning organization and a catalyst for social innovation.

Aligning Family Values

You may have a long history of faith and family traditions which developed your values for giving, but you still need to choose a specific focus for your philanthropy. The key is not to develop your vision/mission in isolation—involve your family and partners too. Had James' grandfather taken this step, his foundation might not be in the position it is in currently.

Determine who these stakeholders are—your spouse or partner, heirs, friends, advisors, colleagues, place of worship or community associations. Get their input on your mission and any research or information you have collected about your cause. Take them through your plan and ask for their feedback. Gather some more information about them while you do so.

- Do they have a favourite cause? Why do they support this?
- What are their objectives for charity?
- Are they consistent with your own?
- Is involving others, like employees or business owners, important to you?

Your stakeholders are invaluable and can become your greatest champions. Make an effort to understand how your philanthropy will be received by your family, friends and community. This is important for a number of reasons. You will want to ensure there is a successor in place to support your cause when you are gone. This will ensure your philanthropy is well placed to stand the test of time. You want to ensure as best you can that no one in your family is resentful about being 'ruled from the grave'.

The sad truth is that people, including family members, can act strangely when a loved one dies. All too often, the courts deal with challenges to wills. By not involving your stakeholders, your chances of a challenge are increased. Involving them up front will require their knowledge of your plans, but it will also mean it is less likely that anyone seeks a claim against your estate. This is why ensuring that you have an up-to-date will is so critically important. In any challenge, the court will want to apply some common sense tests.

- Are the deceased's instructions consistent with what they wanted over a long period of time?
- Is there evidence that the deceased understood the tax implications of their gifting?
- Did the deceased have capacity when he gave those instructions?

Having a documented plan for your philanthropy along with your will can go a long way to ensuring that there will be no objections to your last wishes.

From Family Values to the Values of the Recipient Organization
In order for your gifts to do the good works you intended, you will likely want your recipient organization to be strategic and value-driven as well. But asking tough questions of your chosen charity partners can sometimes be difficult, particularly if you have established a close working relationship with the charity's representatives. That is why it can be worthwhile to include them in your strategic planning. This way they understand up front your granting criteria, recognition wishes and any other conditions you may wish to impose on the gift.

Documenting Your Strategy
Your goals should be articulated in a documented strategic plan for your philanthropy. The plan should include the following components:

- *A mission or strategy statement:* What is your long-term objective? Your statement needs to include three things: "opportunities, competence, and commitment. Every mission statement... has to reflect all three or it will fall down on what is its ultimate goal, its ultimate purpose and final test."[2]
- *Goals:* List your desired goals, and there may be many. List the causes you want to support and specify any areas that you expressly do not want to be involved in.
- *Current situation:* Make a summary of the current problems you are looking to address.
- *Cause:* How did we get here? Describe the causes of the problem and other influencing factors.
- *Alternatives:* What are the options? State the alternative strategies including advantages and disadvantages of each and an estimated cost.

Talking directly to family members about these topics can sometimes be difficult and strain your relationship. If this is a worry, consider engaging an independent third party. Consultants can conduct interviews with each of the key internal (spouse, children and extended family members) and external stakeholders (business partners, your company's executives, plus the charities you are considering supporting) and provide a recommendation report. You can help with the process and be kept in the loop throughout. Once completed, a report should be prepared.

The goal would be for the report to reinforce that your chosen cause is firmly tied to your family's objectives. You can use it to get the series of sign-offs and blessings you need from internal stakeholders to embark. Additionally, funding and budgets for the process and the program could be allocated at this time. This will provide the planning evidence that highlights preferences, objectives, priorities and problems that will guide the development of your giving and help you to develop the longer term plan for your philanthropy.

---

[2]Drucker, Peter. *Managing the Not-for-Profit Organization.* 2005.

Setting Achievable Objectives

What is the difference between setting strategic direction for philanthropy and the setting of objectives? A defined strategy will provide guidance to help you make short- and long-term decisions. However, clear, concise objectives will lead to accountable and achievable action plans for giving, receiving and results. Think of the strategic plan as the environment within which strategic philanthropy is executed. Think of the objectives as the action plan for achieving the results.

Your chances of success—getting the results you want—are greatly increased by setting well-defined goals, including milestones or achievement indicators. Only then can you measure impact of your efforts and on how your philanthropy has made a difference.

So to write effective objectives, you need to think about what you really want to achieve. Are you keen on creating something you can get your family involved in? Do you want to leave a lasting legacy, support your religious beliefs, set an example for others, reciprocate for a good deed done for you, or meet the critical needs of society?

Do Your Research

Start with some initial due diligence. What organizations are doing work in your chosen cause arena? Review the websites of the organizations you are aware of in this space and any materials you can get your hands on. Call them and ask a few questions. You can use the ***Questions you need to ask*** section at the end of this chapter to help you.

Seek Help

Consider other advisors you might turn to for help and/or resources you can access:

- Your financial, legal and accounting advisors
- Philanthropic consultants
- Community and other public foundations
- Other donors

This is just the beginning, but setting strategy and objectives are an important first step in implementing a successful strategic plan for philanthropy. Remember that "strategy is no substitute for good values and passion, but a vehicle for realizing them."[3]

Once you have defined your focus and set your objectives you can move on to select your charities, examine your resources, and determine how, what and when to give, as well as measure the results of your philanthropic giving.

---

[3] Brest, Paul and Harvey, Hal. *Money Well Spent: A Strategic Plan for Smart Philanthropy.* 2008.

IN SUMMARY

There are many ways to help ensure your values are reflected in your philanthropy. It's what matters most to you that is important, as the success story in this chapter will show.

SUCCESS STORY

Judy and Paul Bronfman established their charitable private foundation in 2006. Paul and Judy wanted to carry on the Tzedakah tradition taught to them by their families. The foundation is focused on Jewish organizations, mainly local but most with international reach.

Reaching out to those in need is central to Judaism. "Our desire to make a difference has really been instilled in us from an early age. Both our parents raised us to understand the importance of being charitable. It was expected and not optional. We believe that we are obligated to be compassionate and to give back to those less fortunate than ourselves", Paul explained. "Judy is also very involved with the organizations we support, because for many charities volunteering your time is just as valuable as donating money. Getting people to participate is sometimes the biggest challenge.

"Judy acts as the executive director of the board. Our philanthropy is primarily focused on supporting our community and faith. For us it is important to raise awareness about the growing tide of anti-Semitism in the world today so we focus a lot of our attention on charities with effective programs and strategies that educate against discrimination and bias." Paul and Judy were proud to be honoured for their good work by The Canadian Council for Christians and Jews with the 2008 Human Rights Award.

"Being involved in philanthropy just feels good. It is the right thing to do. And, although our children are not involved in managing our family foundation yet, they accompany us to many charitable events and believe in our cause; they will definitely be involved in the years to come."

THINGS YOU NEED TO KNOW

- Having a well thought-out strategy for your philanthropy greatly increases your chances of success.
- Clear objectives will lead to accountable action plans and the results you want.
- To prepare your strategy and objectives, your family values need alignment and all stakeholders need to be in place.

QUESTIONS YOU NEED TO ASK

- What are the causes I (we) care most about?
- Why do I care about them?
- Does supporting these causes fit my personal values, interest, experience and skills?
- What is the problem I want to address?
- What are the causes of that problem?
- What are the possible solutions?
- What is the environment my cause is operating in?
- What do I want to achieve?
- What charities have I supported in the past?
- Why did I choose to support them?
- What are my expectations in terms of the results?
- What are the risks?

THINGS YOU NEED TO DO

- Start with your internal "family values" review to identify the things that matter most to you.
- Decide who you would like to involve in the development of your plan (e.g. your spouse or partner, heirs, friends, advisors, colleagues).
- Do some preliminary research and due diligence about the causes you wish to support.
- Document your mission and objectives. This will help you establish the criteria for selecting your charities.

DECISIONS YOU NEED TO MAKE

- Find someone to help you research the cause. You may not have time to do all this research, but there are many resources available to help you do so. Consider hiring a consultant to help you.
- Find someone to help you understand the financial and tax consequences of giving.

MASTER YOUR PHILANTHROPY
Develop Your Strategic Plan for Giving

TIPS

- Give responsibly. Be knowledgeable about the causes and organizations you are supporting by doing research.
- Understand the impact you seek.
- Seek advice from informed advisors.
- Document your strategy and objectives—your policy and procedures for family giving.

TRAPS

- Don't get overwhelmed about philanthropy. Your plan can be as simple or complicated as you like. The important thing is to have one.
- Don't try to do this in isolation. Establish a group of stakeholders and advisors to help you.

Principle Mastery: "Strategy is no substitute for good values and passion, but a vehicle for realizing them."[4]

---

[4]Brest, Paul and Harvey, Hal. *Money Well Spent: A Strategic Plan for Smart Philanthropy.* 2008.

CHAPTER 4

Selecting Your Cause

To laugh often and to love much; to win the respect of intelligent persons and the affection of children; to earn the approbation of honest critics and to endure the betrayal of false friends; to appreciate beauty; to find the best in others; to give of oneself; to leave the world a bit better, whether by a healthy child, a garden patch, or a redeemed social condition; to have played and laughed with enthusiasm and sung with exultation; to know that even one life has breathed easier because you have lived—this is to have succeeded.
RALPH WALDO EMERSON

> *Peter has been generously giving all his life. He tends to be a soft touch, responding to telemarketers who have a convincing sales pitch by getting his chequebook out, but he is increasingly disenchanted with this approach. In reacting to requests, he has pursued too many programs and feels that his charitable giving lacks focus. Plus, he isn't sure about the management skills of some of the organizations he has previously supported. They don't seem to be able to articulate their results in a meaningful way. How can he develop a giving strategy so he knows his money is going to legitimate causes and doing the most good?*

THE ISSUES

Giving through the heart is noble, but to build a strategic plan for your philanthropy you must also use your head. Once you've decided where to focus your giving, you need to choose specific charities to support. Your impact will be greatly enhanced if you give to an effective charity. So how can you make sure to choose effective charities and avoid the pitfalls Peter finds himself in? The reality is that for charities, results are sometimes hard to measure.

- How do you find effective charities?
- What questions should you ask on charity visits?
- How do you analyze grant proposals?
- What kind of feedback should you expect from the charity?
- What are the risks that a charity's work will not deliver?[1]

THE SOLUTIONS

Once you have established your goals and objectives, finding the perfect non-profit partner to help you to achieve them is the next step. With 161,000 organizations to choose from, it isn't always easy. There are many organizations out there with worthy missions and good programs, but do they fit with your strategic plan for giving? If you have done a good job in establishing your plan, then you have already made significant progress towards narrowing the field of organizations to focus on. So the next step is to find an effective partner that fits.

Finding Effective Charities

Start your selection process with a review of the organizations doing work in your chosen area. There are likely to be many. So to narrow down the field, set some criteria that the organizations must meet to make your short-list.

---

[1] www.philanthropycapital.org.

- Look for charities that are closely aligned with your chosen priorities.
- Is the organization in good standing with the Canada Revenue Agency? It is important to ensure that the charity has complied with CRA requirements and is in good standing.
- What is the right location for you? Do you want a partner with national or international scope, or do you prefer to focus on your local community or region?

Here is where doing your homework really counts. It is worth spending the time and effort now to ensure that you won't be disappointed later. The number of charities you come up with will depend on the amount of time and effort you are prepared to spend on the research. But you don't need to do it alone. To avoid the paperwork required, consider working with a consultant. There are a number of consultants working in this field who can help you with your research.

Once you have established your short-list, you need to do some desk research. The Canada Revenue Agency publishes the tax returns of every charity in Canada on its website. A lot of information can be gleaned there (e.g., total revenues, the amount the organization spends on fundraising and on management and administrative expenses). To establish evidence of good financial management you should ensure that administrative and fundraising costs are appropriate for the organization. It is important that the organization keep its administrative costs at or below 20% and that the costs of its fundraising activities don't significantly dilute the donations raised. But financial management is not the only measure. You should investigate any website or other public information available from the organization for more information.

Questions to Ask Your Charities

Whether you are approaching the charity for information, or they have approached you with a grant proposal, develop a list of questions. If you can't find the answers you are looking for online, contact the charity by phone or in person to get the answers you need.

- Does the organization clearly articulate its purpose and mandate?
- What is its plan to address the problem it is seeking to solve?

- Is there evidence that they have developed programs that have achieved meaningful results?
- How does the organization explain its achievements and/or evaluate its programs?
- What are the internal capabilities of the organization?
- What evidence can you find of the depth and breadth of the charity?
- Have they been recognized with any awards or developed a new approach to the problem they are looking to solve?
- Based on their experience, are they lobbying for policy change to help the problem they are trying to solve?
- Do they have a website and how extensive is the information they make available (e.g., annual report, publications, newsletters). This will give a good indication of their willingness to be open and transparent with information.
- Who is on their board?
- Do they have volunteers? How many and what do they use them for?

You may wish to speak with one or two members of the board to determine how active the directors are in the charity and their level of awareness of the issues and challenges the charity currently faces. Try to determine how frequently the board receives reports from management and how the charity reports to its donors and other members as well. Are they and the charity they represent credible and do they enjoy a good reputation in their community?

Social responsibility is another important measure to consider. How does the organization affect society through its activities? Many of the measures used to evaluate businesses can also be applied when evaluating your charity.

- Do they support sourcing from sustainable and renewable resources?
- Do they support 'fair trade', ensuring appropriate labour practices?
- What community benefit agreements do they have in place?

Diversification is another element to consider. You may have identified a number of worthy charities that you would like to support, but just like when you are investing you should be careful of over-diversification. A good portfolio is more than a long list of good stocks; it is a balance of protections like cash and bonds with low risk tolerance and opportunities including equities with a higher risk tolerance, but the potential for greater appreciation. Just like with your portfolio, various types of information can be used:

- Does the charity fit with your strategy?
- What is the past performance of the charity and its programs?
- Do the board and its constituents believe in the charity's future prospects?

Analyzing Grant Proposals

Many of the questions apply whether you are considering a donation or analyzing a proposal from your charity for a specific grant to assist a program. However, there are a few additional points to consider in analyzing grant proposals.

- If you are considering funding a specific program, what are the development and ongoing costs?
- If the program already exists, is there evidence that it has achieved meaningful results?
- If the program is new, what are the criteria for success?
- Have they set a timeline for these milestones?

What Kind of Feedback You Should Expect

Remember, you are looking for a partner to whom you will make a significant commitment. If you want to ensure that the relationship you build stands the test of time, you will need to be certain that the people at the charity are well suited to work with you. Once you have identified a charity, you should make sure that your contact there understands your expectations. Ask them to confirm how and with what frequency progress will be monitored and reported back to you, and whether or not you will have access to the decision makers in the organization.

What are the Risks?

Uncertainty is a key feature of investing. There is always an element of risk that you must accept. It is for you to decide what level of risk is acceptable to you, based on your investment knowledge. Assessing the risks of your donations can be treated in a similar fashion. New Philanthropy Capital, a UK-based charity that helps donors and charities to maximize their impact, writes that the "approach (you should take) to charitable giving focuses on investing to deliver results ... to generate a social return on that investment." NPC lists some of those risk-versus-reward scenarios as follows:

- **Strategy and concept:** An untried concept may be risky but have great potential results.
- **Management:** A charity that lacks strong leadership, clarity of vision and management structure is risky. These risks can be controlled by establishing the style, strength and capacity of a charity's management.
- **Operational:** A charity lacking the operational capacity (i.e., processes, staff, systems) to deliver potential results is risky. These risks can be controlled by establishing a charity's capacity in detail in these areas.
- **Financial:** A charity can face many financial risks, such as the loss of a particular funding source. These risks can be mitigated by actively managing funding sources, such as by diversifying funding streams and working to replace funding sources well in advance of them expiring.
- **External:** A charity can face many external risks, based on factors beyond its direct control—such as other organizations or stakeholders, or social, economic or political factors.[2]

---

[2]Lumley, Tris. "Charity Selection." *Philanthropy UK: A Guide to Giving*. 3rd edition.

IN SUMMARY

Whatever your cause, you will want to ensure that the organization you support is being effective. You should ask questions of them and properly analyze any grant proposals they have made. You should make sure they understand your expectations in terms of the kind of feedback and ongoing reporting or communication you would like to have with them. And, it is critical that you understand the risks you are taking in making your donations.

Let's look at how Canadian Crossroads has been effective in helping to stop gender-based violence in Swaziland.

SUCCESS STORY

Canadian Crossroads International's partners in Swaziland work to eradicate violence against women and children.

There is no specific law in Swaziland that criminalizes domestic violence. Gender-based violence is widespread and victims have few legal options. As well, Swazi women are socially and economically dependent on men and may not be able to leave an abusive household.

The Swaziland Action Group Against Abuse (SWAGAA) has worked tirelessly for almost two decades to expose the devastating effects of abuse on women and children in Swaziland and to provide counseling and support to those in need. Canadian Crossroads International (CCI) has worked with SWAGAA for more than 10 years. In 2001 it entered into a partnership to support SWAGAA in stemming the tide of violence against women and children.

In 2004, CCI and SWAGAA initiated a partnership project with the Transition House Association of Nova Scotia (THANS), a network of women's shelters. The partnership is enhancing SWAGAA's counseling services and supporting its efforts to advocate for the rights of women. The partnership with SWAGAA has also exposed THANS to valuable new approaches.

Over the course of the project, Crossroaders have worked with SWAGAA to enhance the organization's long-term strategic planning, program development, advocacy and use of technology. In Canada, SWAGAA staff worked with THANS and other organizations working on violence against women and children. Through these placements, SWAGAA's staff members have explored Canadian strategies in supporting women and children who have experienced abuse and other strategies to tackle gender-based violence, including working with men.

In 2007, CCI secured additional funds to enable SWAGAA to launch a program to work with men. SWAGAA, CCI and THANS are also collaborating with other partners in Southern Africa to strengthen women's leadership in the region through forums, training, exchanges and joint initiatives.[3]

---

[3]Canadian Crossroads International, www.cciorg.ca.

THINGS YOU NEED TO KNOW

- Understand the risks facing your charity which may impact your gift: strategy and concept, management, operational, financial, and external.

QUESTIONS YOU NEED TO ASK

- Does the organization clearly articulate its purpose and mandate?
- What is its plan to address the problem it is seeking to solve?
- Is there evidence that they have developed programs that have achieved meaningful results?
- How does the organization explain its achievements and/or evaluate its programs?
- And the other questions outlined in this chapter…

THINGS YOU NEED TO DO

- Make sure your charity understands your expectations in terms of granting the gift and in terms of reporting back to you on their progress.
- Assessing the robustness of an organization's strategies and its capacity to carry them out is an essential aspect of the due-diligence process, and so is coming to judgment about the risks involved.[4]

DECISIONS YOU NEED TO MAKE

- Decide if one charity is enough, or if you need to diversify and give to several organizations to achieve your goals.

---

[4]Brest, Paul and Harvey, Hal. *Money Well Spent: A Strategic Plan for Smart Philanthropy.* 2008.

MASTER YOUR PHILANTHROPY
Selecting Your Cause

TIPS

- Establish some selection criteria and assess your candidates against those criteria.
- Evaluate the risk/return scenarios to ensure your donation will generate a social return.

TRAPS

- Be careful not to over-diversify and dilute your impact.
- Make sure your charity understands your expectations before you give.

Principle Mastery: Remember, you are looking for a partner to whom you will make a significant commitment. If you want to ensure that the relationship you build stands the test of time, you will need to be certain that the people at the charity are well suited to work with you.

CHAPTER 5

Ways to Give

Do all the good you can, by all the means you can,
In all the ways you can, in all the places you can,
At all the times you can, to all the people you can,
As long as ever you can. JOHN WESLEY

> John and Kerry were business owners and, having started and sustained their own business for years, they wanted to be able to help support entrepreneurs in their community to get started. They contacted the Canadian Youth Business Foundation (CYBF), a national charity dedicated to growing Canada's economy one young entrepreneur at a time. Partnering with CYBF would enable them to assist young entrepreneurs by providing coaches for pre-launch advice, start-up financing, and mentoring and business resources along the way.
>
> But this wasn't their only passion. They had other interests, particularly the performing arts in their community, where there were a number of small not-for-profits that they wanted to support too. The problem was time. They were still working and they liked to spend any free time they had on the golf course.

How can John and Kerry support all the causes they care about without having to field regular calls and make visits, as well as keep up with the administration of their gifts? Should they continue to give directly to charities or should they give through a public foundation? Or should they consider establishing a private foundation of their own?

THE ISSUES

Having established your strategy and selected your charities, your next step is to determine the method of your giving. There are many approaches you might choose for your philanthropy, including some that allow you to combine financial and social returns. John and Kerry need to decide if giving directly or indirectly is the best approach for them. There are many ways to give. Let's explore them now. There's sure to be a way that suits you.

THE SOLUTIONS

Giving Directly or Indirectly

You can choose to be involved directly with the charities you have selected or to give indirectly (for example, through a foundation) via endowments and donor-advised funds.

Giving directly ensures you have direct contact with the charities carrying out the charitable activities and direct communication from them relating to their activities. But having direct contact with organizations sometimes can be difficult, especially if you impose conditions on your gift. You will also have to do all the paperwork relating to your gifts yourself unless you hire an administrator.

An alternative is to use a community or national public foundation like Benefaction and set up a personal endowment or donor-advised fund. In this case, the foundation supports the good work of other charities. Its staff can negotiate granting criteria on your behalf and ensure that you get recognition for your gift, if you wish it. For busy people, this is an effective and low-cost solution that still allows you to decide who will receive your gifts. You can focus on your giving, keep administration costs down and avoid getting bogged down in paperwork.

Giving Time and Skills

Many charities are under-resourced and some lack the business skills needed to help them grow and manage their organization and programs effectively. Sometimes, donating your time and business acumen can be as valuable to charities as financial donations.

Charities often deal with a difficult balancing act. Increasingly, donors are putting conditions on their gifts, preferring to support a new initiative that they believe will have the greatest impact, instead of allowing their donations to fund core costs such as management salaries and administration. The charities are then constrained in what they may do with the donations.

So, "charities can find themselves stretching the parameters of their mission and expertise to secure the funding they need to keep experienced staff. They are often responsible for helping vulnerable people and juggling multiple income sources to stay operational. They therefore often struggle to find time to plan for a more secure future. Volunteers with business skills can teach charity managers the skills, tools and approaches they use in their working lives to help them plan for stability, efficiency and growth."[1]

Setting up a New Charity

Another way to give is to set up your own private foundation. This is an effective route if you want to maintain control over your activities, but it can be expensive and time consuming. Also, with over 9,000 public and private foundations in place, it is likely that there is already a charity with a similar mandate to your own. You should investigate this before committing to the set-up costs. An existing charity may be happy to

---

[1] Xavier, Deborah. "Giving Time." *Philanthropy UK: A Guide to Giving.* 3rd edition.

carry out the work you specify, based on an endowment gift. Private foundations are really most effective for sums over $5 million, assuming you are prepared to do the work required. For smaller amounts, an endowment or donor-advised fund with a public charity is a far simpler and more cost-effective solution.

If a private foundation is your choice, you will need to establish a board of directors, decide on your corporate structure (trust or incorporation, national or provincial) and process that application. Then, you need to apply for charitable registration with the Canada Revenue Agency. On an ongoing basis, you will need to hold regular meetings, keep minutes, issue tax receipts, keep adequate books and records, report to the CRA and administer your grants and monitor your annual budget. And, you may be audited. Usually some professional staff is needed.

In Canada, a charity must qualify as being charitable under one of four specific categories:

- The relief of poverty;
- The advancement of education;
- The advancement of religion;
- And other purposes beneficial to the community as a whole in a way the law regards as charitable.

In addition, to qualify for registration as a charity, an organization must meet a "public benefit" test. An organization must show that its purposes and activities provide a tangible benefit to the public as a whole or a significant section of it. All this is done at the outset when you establish the objectives of your organization in its charter.

Maximizing Social Return

Increasingly, philanthropists are looking for ways to combine both financial and social returns, and they want their resources to achieve the greatest possible impact. Many methods have evolved to help them do this. Below are brief descriptions of a few that you might want to consider.

Social entrepreneurs look for a variety of returns, but the financial return may be secondary to social or environmental ones. They are typically "entrepreneurial" or business-like in approaching their work to solve social problems on a large scale.[2] While the phenomenon of social enterprises and entrepreneurs is not new, it is growing and increasingly relevant with supporters like the Schwab Foundation for Social Entrepreneurship. It financially supports selected social entrepreneurs of its network to participate in the various events and initiatives of the World Economic Forum, providing them with an opportunity to draw on the support, the knowledge and the networks of its members and constituents.

Venture philanthropy uses a business approach of venture capital to fund a social mandate. A venture philanthropist takes a long-term investment approach to giving, supporting with capital as well as management expertise. Key characteristics of venture philanthropy according to the European Venture Philanthropy Association are:

- The active partnership, or engagement, of donors, volunteers and/or experts with charities to achieve agreed outcomes such as organizational effectiveness, capacity building or other important change.
- The use of a variety of financing techniques in addition to grants, such as multi-year financing, loans or other financial instruments most appropriate for a charity's needs.
- The capability to provide skills and/or hands-on resources with the objective of adding value to the development of a charity.
- The desire to enable donors to maximize the social return on their investment, whether that be as a financial donor or as a volunteer of time and expertise.

There are number of organizations devoted to social entrepreneurship and venture philanthropy in Canada. For example, Social Capital Partners (SCP) arranges for growth financing and provides advisory services to successful businesses that integrate a social mission into their human resources model and expand career opportunities for disadvantaged

---

[2]Edwards, Michael. *Just Another Emperor? The Myths and Realities of Philanthrocapitalism.* D-emos. 2008.

populations. SCP works with all types of corporate structures—for-profit, nonprofit, charitable—and the key to accessing loan capital is the commitment to hire an agreed-upon number of employees over a certain timeframe, from employment programs serving people with barriers to employment.

Microfinancing organizations "provide financial services to people on low incomes who do not have access to credit and other financial services. While the services and products vary, microfinancing organizations typically make small loans (of around $100) to poor people for short periods of time. The original premise of microfinance was that people who were traditionally excluded from the banking sector because of lack of income or collateral could borrow to meet their credit needs. These needs either go unmet or are met at the exorbitant terms set by money-lenders. The concept was bolstered by Muhammed Yunnis and the Grameen Bank jointly winning the Nobel Peace Prize in 2006 for their 'efforts to create economic and social development from below,' and a United Nations Year to champion the movement in 2005."[3] In Canada, there are a number of organizations involved in microfinancing, including Opportunity International and Canadian Crossroads International.

Socially responsible investment (SRI) is also on the rise in Canada. "84% of Canadians think financial analysts should incorporate social and environmental performance when they value a company's shares," according to GlobeScan 2007. SRI combines a company's financial performance with a review of its impact on the environment or the people it affects. It seeks to ensure there is no trade-off between financial performance and social responsibility—and to promote more sustainable companies over the long term. There is mounting evidence of our consensus on environmental and social issues as SRI funds take an increasing share of the investment market in Canada and around the world.

---

[3] Whitni, Thomas. "Micro-finance." *Philanthropy UK: A Guide to Giving.* 3rd edition.

IN SUMMARY

Determining how you are going to make your gift is an important element of your strategic plan. You must figure out what is required to make a real difference, and then, based on your resources, decide on your method. Your choice will also depend on your goals and the effectiveness of the existing charities supporting the causes you value.

You'll need to determine how much of a role you want to play and whether or not you wish to fund a specific program or trust the charity to balance program funding and general operating expenses.

SUCCESS STORY

W. Brett Wilson, a successful Canadian entrepreneur and TV personality, channels his philanthropy in a number of ways.

"I agree with Mother Teresa who said, 'No gift is too small.' Whether you donate your time, your talent or your money, the important thing is that you get involved and give back. I learned the value of giving back from my parents, who didn't have a lot of money, but gave of their time and encouraged others to do the same. They inspired leadership and rarely turned anyone down. My father was a coach for most teams that my sisters and I played on and would walk door to door for the United Way and other causes. My mother couldn't swim, but she once put on a life jacket and swam 40 laps for charity. They paved a path for me.

"I wouldn't say that I have a master plan for my philanthropy. I have given to organizations in six countries in Africa and built houses in Mexico, but for the bulk of the work I do, I keep my focus on Alberta and Saskatchewan. I give both time and money toward health care initiatives, especially profiling the importance of early screening for prostate cancer, which nearly took my life a few years back; I have a passion for promoting entrepreneurship; I have supported programs that deal with the root causes of domestic violence; and I am actively promoting the sports of volleyball and swimming.

"I'm always looking for ways to be innovative in my giving, especially through creative partnerships or high-profile public events. I've used charitable events to support various community initiatives. The 50th birthday party I organized in 2007 with a group of friends who were all hitting that same milestone is probably the most successful so far. We invited over 1500 guests to enjoy a concert with Randy Bachman and Burton Cummings, Herman's Hermits, and Beverley Mahood. Everybody dressed up in clothes from their favourite decade and enjoyed comfort food like mac and cheese. The event was more than just fun, as the 'price of admission' was a 'meaningful' charity cheque. We raised $3 million for prostate cancer awareness that night—the biggest single-night fundraiser in Calgary's history.

"I'm a busy person, and I give to many organizations, so establishing a family fund at the Calgary Foundation was an effective way to give because they do all the administration. We have several funds set up at TCF, and my whole family gets involved in determining where their portion of the funds' annual grants will go.

"My advice to charities is to do their homework and understand what is relevant to the donor before making a request. Charities also have to be able to communicate what they are doing succinctly (I ask for one page letters) and I have been known to leverage my donations by offering matching gifts—$1.00 for every $1.00 they can raise themselves. When I challenged my hometown of North Battleford, Saskatchewan with a matching gift of $300,000, they didn't think they would be able to hit that target. But the whole town rallied behind the cause, raising $500,000 for technological improvements to the local hospital, which I matched. In the process, they learned what they were really capable of achieving."

THINGS YOU NEED TO KNOW

- Your time can be as valuable a donation as money because many charities are under-resourced and lack business skills.
- There is a lot of work associated with running your own private foundation.
- Endowment gifts and donor-advised funds can be effective, low-cost ways to give, but keep you in control of where your gifts ultimately go.

QUESTIONS YOU NEED TO ASK

- Do you want to play an active role?
- Do I want to be involved directly with these charities?
- Should I hire a consultant or administrator?
- How much time can you devote?

THINGS YOU NEED TO DO

- Look for ways to combine financial and social returns to achieve the greatest impact.

DECISIONS YOU NEED TO MAKE

- Determine your method for giving—directly or indirectly.

MASTER YOUR PHILANTHROPY
Ways to Give

TIPS

- Brett Wilson's tip: *"There is so much people can do. No matter how much you can afford to give, open your chequebook and give it. Or give of your time. You will provide leadership and inspire others."*
- Look for ways to combine financial and social returns to achieve the greatest impact.

TRAPS

- Be careful not to hamstring your charity with too many gift conditions. Make sure they are not stretched to balance program funding vs. administration expenses.

Principle Mastery: Determine what is required for you to make a real difference for your cause. Understand the level of involvement you want. Then decide whether to give directly to a charity or indirectly through a public or private foundation.

CHAPTER 6

Family Business and Philanthropy

One of the most misunderstood things about business is that people are either doing things for altruistic reasons or they are greedy and selfish, just after profit. That type of dichotomy portrays a false image of business. The whole idea is to do both. JOHN MACKEY

Robert needed to adjust his focus. He was at 58 still heavily involved in his family's successful lumber business. He had toyed with the idea of selling, but his work was a real joy for him especially because he got to see his young sons and daughter almost every day. He wanted to pass on his business successfully in time, but also to be able to spend more time addressing his other passion—nature conservation. Robert owned extensive lands and he had chosen the Nature Conservancy of Canada (NCC), Canada's leading national land conservation organization as his charitable partner in protecting Canada's priority natural areas. But there was a problem. How could Robert increase his commitment to helping his cause while continuing to run a business?

THE ISSUES

In earlier chapters of this book we discussed how to develop your strategy for philanthropy and select your cause. This approach remains sound when determining a philanthropic strategy for your business because your business philanthropy will stem from personal and family values. You could also consider holding family council meetings to develop the strategy. Once you have done that, there are still a few more considerations in developing your corporate philanthropic strategy.

This concept of corporate social responsibility (CSR) can be defined in many ways. Companies practicing CSR connect to social and/or environmental goals through their business. This can consist of corporate philanthropy (company giving and volunteering), or it can consist of a company's use of what is called "triple-bottom-line accounting". Triple-bottom-line accounting captures an expanded spectrum of values and criteria for measuring organizational (and societal) success—looking at economic, ecological and social outcomes of all of its activities including advertising and lobbying. (Shell was the first major company to publish a social report in 1998).[1]

However you define it, corporations are dealing with an increasingly informed and educated general public by incorporating CSR into their core business activities.[2] The demand for corporate accountability continues. What began as risk management in response to anti-corporate activism has evolved into companies keen to monitor the impact of their operations and/or try to enhance their brand and improve their standing in their communities. Some have questioned whether CSR is really just a public relations exercise, but there are many businesses large and small that embrace the need to manage their environmental footprint, avoid producing goods that kill or exploit, obey the regulations imposed by government to secure the public interest, or contribute to their community by providing training and education.

Unfortunately, there aren't enough of them. In 2006 Canadian corporations gave $1.7 billion collectively, compared to individual donations of

---

[1] Edwards, Michael. *Just another Emperor?* 2008.
[2] November 2006 "What's Wrong with Corporate Social Responsibility?" Corporate Watch.

$8.4 billion. According to Imagine Canada, 79% of large companies have a regular and ongoing program for charitable contributions, but large organizations give just 1% of their pre-tax profit away. Overall, only 22% of businesses in Canada give regular charitable contributions, only 8% of them have a written policy regarding their contributions and just 13% measure the benefits of the contributions they make. Why? Some argue that it is not up to the companies to give their money away because public corporations are responsible to their shareholders. But now more than ever, in the face of government funding cutbacks, it is important for companies to step in and fill that gap. Imagine Canada's 2008 survey findings are encouraging. Their 2008 study of Canada's largest corporations told us that the philanthropic spirit is alive and well among the corporations in Canada with the deepest pockets and that these same companies would do better if they were more organized and strategic, on the lookout for opportunities to work with a broader array of charities, and better able to measure the tangible benefits associated with their philanthropy.

THE SOLUTIONS

Just like for individual giving, for companies to give effectively—and sustainably—they must make a plan and then stick to it with informed choices. There are some other important issues to consider:

- Create a giving strategy that complements your business mission.
- Define your budget.
- Create awareness of your giving through public relations.
- Engage your employees and your family.
- Maximize your gifts and minimize your taxes.

Ensure your strategy complements your business mission

It just makes sense to ensure your giving strategy complements your family business mission and values, as Robert did when he chose to ensure that his family's success was not achieved at the cost of depleting Canada's natural resources. In return for making a difference in your community, you can also produce returns for your company, but there are a few additional considerations for business owners developing a strategic plan for philanthropy, as outlined by Allison & Partners, a US public relations firm.[3]

- Consider whether your company's mission and your customers and community already fit in a specific charity niche. Does your company already put a premium on good corporate citizenship?
- What are your business objectives for the year? (i.e. sales objectives, store traffic)
- Do you feel that involving employees in the community is important?

In addition to the solutions from chapter 2, your answers to these questions should be considered during the development of your strategy. You should also determine who within your organization should be making the decisions about where you donate. It could be the business owner, or it could be a committee of executives or employees.

Define your budget

There are a couple of common approaches to budgeting for charitable giving. You could establish a certain percentage of pre-tax profit and donate that each year. Or, you could develop an annual budget to support a specific program that you wish to support.

If you choose the latter, the budget for the program could become part of the corporate financial plan. The Calgary Foundation suggests that, in formulating the budget each year, you should take into account issues such as:

- Requirements of program strategy and plans,
- Current revenue and profit projections,
- Availability of other resources,
- Internal competition for resources, and
- Spending patterns of other companies in this area.[4]

---

[3]Pansky, Scott. *Cause 101: A Toolbox for Business.* Allison & Partners. San Francisco, 2005.
[4]The Calgary Foundation. *Creating a Giving Program: A guide for small and mid-sized companies.*

Create awareness

Communication is very important because good communications to the right audience will help to ensure your success. There are traditional ways to do this including issuing a press release, getting to know local reporters and helping them with good story ideas, sponsorship, advertising and online marketing. But sponsoring an event or just putting your logo on a package isn't enough. Once you have established your strategy and selected your charities, consider creating a communications plan that will work for you. By identifying your key messages and aiming them at the right target audiences using the right types of media, you can create a cause-related marketing and/or community relations program that makes a difference, is strategic, and is grounded in accountability for your company.[5]

Engage your employees

Employees want to be associated with a company that is doing good things in the community. Having your own community-related program can help you to attract and retain committed employees. You may not wish to involve your employees in your philanthropy, but doing so allows you to leverage that commitment and create an even bigger impact for your cause.

Consider a matching program where your company matches your employees' donations to your charitable organization dollar for dollar. You should set some limits on the amount you will match and on the type of charitable organizations you will support. Alternatively, challenge your employees to raise funds from other sources within a set period of time and match your company's gift, or loan your employees expertise out to help a charity with an event or program. You should involve your human relations experts in the process.

Maximize your gift, minimize your tax

Both tax credits and deductions are good things for taxpayers. Any tax credit reduces an individual's tax payable or owing. A deduction reduces

---

[5]Pansky, Scott. *Cause 101: A Toolbox for Business*. Allison & Partners. San Francisco, 2005.

taxable income for either companies or individuals. In terms of donations in Canada, they are treated as donations for individuals but for companies donations are treated as deductions.

So, if your company gives to charity, you are permitted to use the donation to reduce your income just like any other expense. However, unlike other expenses, you can use the charitable contribution (up to 75% of income) in the year of the gift or in any of the next five years. It might be more advantageous for owners to give through their company than rather than making personal donations. You should consider donations of public and private securities through your private corporations. Examples of this are provided in Chapter 2.

Involve family members who aren't in the business

In addition to being good for business and responding to social needs, your company's philanthropy can keep your family together in other ways, especially those who are not involved in the business. Mark Evans, Head of Family Business at Coutts & Co. in the UK writes, "One way family businesses do this is to set up a family trust (or fund) and donate a percentage of pre-tax profits to the trust. Family philanthropy can also be used to teach the next generation the value of money and can provide a new sense of purpose to family members leaving the business. Not to mention that it can be among the most enjoyable and rewarding things a family can do.[6]

---

[6]Evans, Mark. *Philanthropy UK: A Guide to Giving*, 3rd edition.

IN SUMMARY

Many families and family businesses give back to their communities because it is the right thing to do. In fact, investing in social capital is one characteristic of long-lasting businesses. Families that invest in the community around them, whether local, provincial or national, receive many benefits in return.

SUCCESS STORY

Owner James Epp spoke at an awards dinner held September 19, 2007 where he was recognized for his charitable giving. The following is an excerpt from his speech.

"Vanessa and I own a number of companies with locations across Canada. Our business is manufacturing, selling, renting and servicing recreational vehicles. In 1969 my family moved from the prairies to Abbotsford, BC, where Dad purchased a small camper manufacturing business. School was not of much interest to me; however, it was at work where I learned from those around me and most of all from my father.

"I was blessed by my parents' long-term vision, not only with business but also with their faith. Dad, who always was at the bank borrowing for another expansion or piece of equipment, also was on our church board and building committee when there was a key church expansion, and Dad, along with four other men, guaranteed the financial package. Without access to a large amount of cash to back up his commitments, Dad sent my mother to the credit union to borrow money to help with the church building project. This was the norm not the exception.

"In 1980 Dad and I, on short notice, flew to Penticton on a last minute charter. We heard the night before that Trav L Mate, an RV manufacturer, was selling off its assets. This small manufacturer offered a variety of inventory and equipment. After the purchase, some negotiation with key staff and a new bank, we re-opened the Penticton plant. Shortly after Dad decided he would set up office in Penticton and I took on the Abbotsford operation. What an opportunity!

"In 1983 Dad brought my younger brother in as a partner in Penticton and sold the Abbotsford operation to Vanessa and me, leasing the property to us. The leasing company included my sister, Brenda. As I look back I'm amazed at how Dad planned for the succession of his business and today I'm thankful for the relationship I have with my brother and sister. From 1983 to today our business has grown from 25 employees to over 300, from one location to 10 locations. I have been blessed with dedicated long-term employees. Opportunities for growth continue to come our way. Now the bank asks us, "Where do you want to expand?"

"A few years ago I sensed the need to adjust my focus and I toyed with the idea of selling the business or pulling back the reins of growth. But there was a problem. How could I increase my commitment to helping others while running a business? I joined a group of Christian businessmen, called BBL (Beyond the Bottom Line). As well, I consulted with (my financial advisors) and have drawn from the wisdom of these men.

I began to understand that as an entrepreneur I need to use the talent and resources I have been given and recognize that our business is the mission where God has placed me. With this renewed focus I have committed to strategically grow our company with the plan to develop a leadership team to take the responsibility for the operation. This should allow for flexibility in my life to fulfill what I understand is my calling, business with a mission.

"I have always been skeptical of any tax saving schemes. However, after considerable due diligence, I agreed to look deeper into an opportunity presented by the Legacy Foundation. I consulted with our accountants and a credible law firm from Vancouver and after receiving a green light from them I preceded with our agreement. (It)...fit well in our succession plan. I would encourage all those who have a heart to save more and seek the opportunity to give more, to look into the Legacy Philanthropy Model. The excitement of operating a successful business will always be there but clearly comes second to allowing God to use it for His purpose.[7]

---

[7] Legacy Foundation. www.legacyofcanada.net, Featured Stories, Business Owners.

THINGS YOU NEED TO KNOW

- Building goodwill in the community can sustain and protect your business in a time of crisis.
- Corporate philanthropy can be an expression of the culture of the company.
- Giving enhances your company reputation and is good for business and brand building.
- Employees want to be associated with a company that is helping its community. Your giving can help make you better able to attract and retain employees.
- Corporate giving can involve more than just money. Time and expertise can also be gifts.
- Because they are good citizens, caring businesses are considered by government and community officials when policy decisions are being made.

QUESTIONS YOU NEED TO ASK

- Do your company mission and the company's target audience already fit in a specific charity niche?
- Which members of the family and the business should be involved in managing your charitable giving?

THINGS YOU NEED TO DO

- Develop a communications strategy to create awareness.
- Seek advice to determine your best strategy to maximize giving while minimizing your tax burden.

DECISIONS YOU NEED TO MAKE

- How will you engage your employees in your philanthropy?
- Should you consider a cause-related marketing program for your corporate gifting?

MASTER YOUR PHILANTHROPY
Family Business and Philanthropy

TIPS

- Ensure your strategy complements your business mission.
- Create awareness.
- Engage your employees.
- Involve family members.

TRAPS

- Avoid chequebook giving. Ensure your giving strategy complements your family business mission and values.

Principle Mastery: Companies that do better at philanthropy than their peers are more organized and strategic, on the lookout for opportunities to work with a broader array of charities, and better able to measure the tangible benefits associated with their philanthropy.

CHAPTER 7

Grant Making and Foundation Management

As the funds you will expend have come from many places in the world, so let there be no territorial, religious, or color restrictions on your benefactions, but beware of organized, professional charities with high-salaried executives and a heavy ratio of expense. CONRAD HILTON

> Susan was recently appointed treasurer of a local charity helping children in need, but to her dismay in her first week on the job she learned that the CRA had revoked the charity's status. Her predecessor had failed to file its tax return on time and there were problems with the organization's finances. Based on the donation receipts, their annual disbursement quota amounted to more than the organization had in liquid assets. They had overspent on administration. How could the Board have allowed this to happen?

THE ISSUES

Grant-making and foundation management are important responsibilities. If you are a director of a charitable organization, or you are thinking about getting involved in doing so, there are many issues to consider. Earlier in this book, we discussed setting objectives. In addition to establishing the charity's purpose, there are some other questions you will want to answer.

- What is the legal status and registration of the charity?
- What is my role as a fiduciary?
- What are the disbursement quota requirements?
- Is the charity in good standing with the CRA?
- How are the charity's assets being managed?
- What policies has the board put in place to safeguard the organization?

To help to answer these important questions, let's explore some of the rules for charities around grant-making, grant funding and board governance.

THE SOLUTIONS

Legal Status and Registration

There are two legal structures for charitable foundations: trusts and not-for-profit (NFP) corporations. Historically, trusts were the most common form of charitable organization. They are relatively easy to establish and do not require registration other than with Canada Revenue Agency. However, today NFP corporations are more prevalent. The reason for this lies in the fact that a trust has no separate legal status apart from the trustee(s). As a result, a trustee is personally liable for his or her actions in relation to the trust. NFP corporations on the other hand have a clearly defined legal status; objectives are articulated in their charters, they can continue to exist when directors or members move on, and directors have limited liability.

Either way, directors and trustees are responsible to ensure that the organization complies with its reporting and granting requirements. The nature of these requirements depends on the type of registration of the organization. There are three types of registration or status assigned to a charity by CRA—charitable organizations, public foundations and private foundations. Charitable organizations are those that are directly involved in doing good work. Other criteria for status as a charitable organization include organizations that:

- devote all resources to charitable activities that it carries on itself;
- do not pay any part of its income to the personal benefit of any director or member;
- have more than 50% of its directors dealing at arm's length with each other;
- are not controlled by a person who has contributed over 50% of the organization's funding or by a person who is not at arm's length.[1]

Foundations differ from charitable organizations in that they are formed for the purpose of funding other charities. A public foundation, like a charitable organization, must have more than 50% of directors at arm's length and it may not receive more than 50% of income from one source. A private foundation, however, may be privately controlled and/or funded, and it may either carry on its own charitable activities and/or it may fund other qualified donees, such as other registered charities. In each case, a director does take on fiduciary responsibilities.

Fiduciary Responsibility

A fiduciary is a legal term describing a person to whom property or power is entrusted for the benefit of another. Their role is based on one of trust and confidence. Specific responsibilities differ depending on the legal structure and registration of the organization, but whether a trustee or a director of a NFP corporation, there are a number of common areas of concern. A fiduciary is expected to act in the best interests of the organization and may not profit personally from the relationship or receive remuneration except for reimbursement of reasonable expenses.

---

[1]Canada Revenue Agency, T4063 – *Registering a Charity for Income Tax Purposes*, 2008.

A fiduciary is obliged to act prudently and manage the affairs of the organization as he would his own. Susan was now facing the task of educating her own board about their responsibilities.

Disbursement Quota (DQ)

The DQ is the minimum amount that a registered charity is required to spend each year on its own charitable programs, or on gifts to qualified donees. The purpose of the DQ is to ensure that most of a charity's funds are used to further its charitable purposes and activities. Charities are discouraged from accumulating excessive funds, and they are expected to keep other expenses at a reasonable level.

The DQ is largely based on what happened in the previous fiscal period. The current annual disbursement quota is made up of a number of components:

- 80% of donations received in the previous fiscal year;
- 80% (100% for private foundations) of amounts received from other registered charities in the previous year;
- 3.5% of the average value of assets owned not used directly in charitable activities or administration in the 24 months prior to the current fiscal period (e.g. endowments and other restricted assets).

Investment Management

Directors and trustees of foundations are entrusted with primary fiduciary responsibilities on behalf of the organization and it is their job to manage the foundation's assets wisely. This is an increasingly demanding task with more requests for grants and, in times of turbulent markets, possible decreasing returns on investments. Balancing the requirements of grant-making versus growing investment assets for the long term is the challenge. In a period of lower returns, capital can be eroded if the investment income does not sufficiently keep up with or exceed the minimum spending needs. Many boards will delegate the responsibility for managing the foundation's assets to a professional investment manager who can help them to manage the disbursement quota requirement.[2]

---

[2] HSBC Asset Management Canada Ltd., *Foundation Management in Canada: An Introduction for Trustees*, 2002.

Forms of Grant Funding

Whatever your budget for granting is in a given year, there are really two ways to make that funding available to your chosen charities. One is to provide donations for general operating expenses. The other is to provide donations with a condition—for example, that the donation must be used to fund a specific project or program. Either way, good fundraisers will make sure that you give where you want and that you understand what your gift will do for the organization.

The distinction is an important one. If you believe that the organization is well-managed, focused and closely aligned to your goals, it can often be better to let them decide where to put the money. They are, after all, the experts on the ground. However, if you have questions around how your dollars might be used, or if you want to ensure that your money goes directly to fund a specific initiative and is not allocated to general administration, then placing a condition on the gift is a better bet.

Policy Governance

One way to establish whether the organization you are planning to support is effective is to look to the board. The role of the board is to govern the organization in an organized, planned and disciplined manner. In terms of governance, it is a good idea to ensure the directors understand their deliverables. A leading model on best practice for boards can be found in Dr. John Carver's Policy Governance® Model. It describes a process designed to empower boards of directors to fulfill their obligations of accountability for the organizations they govern as follows:

"As a generic system, the Policy Governance Model is applicable to the governing body of any enterprise. The model enables the board to focus on the larger issues, to delegate with clarity, to control management's job without meddling, to rigorously evaluate the accomplishment of the organization, to truly lead its organization.

"In contrast to the approaches typically used by boards, Policy Governance separates issues of organizational purpose (ENDS) from all other organizational issues (MEANS), placing primary importance on those Ends. Policy Governance boards demand accomplishment of purpose, and only limit the

staff's available means to those which do not violate the board's pre-stated standards of prudence and ethics.

"The board's own Means are defined in accordance with the roles of the board, its members, the chair and other officers, and any committees the board may need to help it accomplish its job. This includes the necessity to 'speak with one voice'. Dissent is expressed during the discussion preceding a vote. Once (a vote is) taken, the board's decisions may subsequently be changed, but are never to be undermined. The board's expectations for itself also set out self-imposed rules regarding the delegation of authority to the staff and the method by which board-stated criteria will be used for evaluation. Policy Governance boards delegate with care. There is no confusion about who is responsible to the board or for what board expectations they are responsible. Double delegation (for example, to a board committee as well as to the CEO) is eliminated. Furthermore, boards that decide to utilize a CEO function are able to hold this one position exclusively accountable.

"Evaluation, with such carefully stated expectations, is nothing more than seeking an answer to the question, 'Have our expectations been met?' The board, having clarified its expectations, can assess performance in that light. This focused approach reduces the mountains of paperwork boards often feel obliged to review. Moreover, those boards which worry that they are only furnished the data management wants to give them find that, in stating their expectations and demanding a relevant and credible accounting of performance, they have effectively taken over control of their major information needs. Their staff no longer has to read their minds.

"Policy Governance is a radical and effective change in the way boards conceive of and do their job. It allows greater accountability. Board leadership isn't just rhetoric. It's a reality."[3]

---

[3]Carver, John. *The Policy Governance Model*, www.carvergovernance.com

IN SUMMARY

The purpose for any board of directors is to be accountable that its organization works. This means that the board is responsible to ensure that the organization accomplishes the intended results as expressed in its mission statement at the intended cost. It also means ensuring that the organization avoids unacceptable methods, conduct, activities and circumstances. The executive director or CEO is responsible and should not allow the finances of the organization to come into jeopardy or accept a material deviation of actual expenditures from the budget and priorities established by the board. Had Susan's board clearly defined the parameters around which its executives could act with specific limitation policies, its current dilemma may have been avoided.

SUCCESS STORY

Ruth M. Grant has a life-long history of philanthropy. She is a past chair of the United Way, a past chair of SickKids Foundation and vice chair of the SickKids Hospital, and she is the chair of HealthyKids International, a groundbreaking initiative designed to transform children's healthcare on a global scale. HealthyKids International supports the sharing of knowledge among the world's best pediatric specialists, with the goals of improving children's health, helping build capacity, and ensuring that this wealth of knowledge is sustainable through strategic resourcing.

Ruth explains that she has watched Canada's charitable sector evolve "slowly but surely."

"Governance was a key issue for many organizations across Canada in the mid 90s. It became increasingly important to ensure the organization had a strategic plan and that it had the right set of skills on the board to set that plan in motion. Board directors need to understand their role, be good stewards of donor dollars and be open and transparent as part of their accountability. Unfortunately, not all organizations are as far along as they should be. The board is responsible for the hiring, monitoring and, if need be, firing of the executive director or CEO. Not all organizations have that relationship clear."

In terms of how donors and charities work together, there is good news. From Ruth's perspective, this increased transparency and accountability are good things.

"I see that the government is recommending that costs to raise donor dollars should not exceed 35%. That is a good target and it is manageable. It does cost to raise money, and events, lotteries, and community-type fundraisers are often the most expensive. Nonetheless, they are an important part of community building and awareness. Major gifts cost very little in comparison, so fundraising should be a mix of all types so that the 35% benchmark is not exceeded."

Ruth is pleased with what she and her husband have invested in.

"I am thankful that we can afford to do so and I would encourage more people to donate to causes dear to them. I believe that those to whom much is given, much is expected. Some can give time, some talent and some treasure and, in some cases, all three! But the community is only as strong as its philanthropic spirit. Civic society depends on the involvement of its citizenry—the challenge is to inspire people to make a contribution in whatever way they can."

THINGS YOU NEED TO KNOW

- There are two legal structures for charitable foundations: trusts and NFP corporations.
- There are three types of charitable status: charitable organizations, public foundations and private foundations.
- Directors and trustees of charities have fiduciary responsibilities.

QUESTIONS YOU NEED TO ASK

- What is the legal status and registration of the charity?
- What is my role as a fiduciary?
- What are the disbursement quota requirements?
- Is the charity in good standing with the CRA?
- How are the charity's assets being managed?
- What policies has the board put in place to safeguard the organization?

THINGS YOU NEED TO DO

- As a board member, make sure you hire the right people with the skills to manage the foundation and its finances.

DECISIONS YOU NEED TO MAKE

- Determine whether to put conditions on your gifts.

MASTER YOUR PHILANTHROPY
Grant Making and Foundation Management

TIPS

- Clarifying your expectations as a board member will help you to assess the performance of a charity's staff and help them to account for and report on their performance better.

TRAPS

- Be wary of fundraisers that cannot clearly explain where your donation dollars will be spent and what your gift will do for the organization.

Principle Mastery: Effective boards understand their responsibilities to their organizations and inform themselves about investment, accounting and legal matters that are crucial to ongoing financial success.

CHAPTER 8

Monitor and Evaluate Your Impact

Philanthropy is all about making a positive difference in the world by devoting your resources and your time to causes you believe in. In my case, I like to support causes where "a lot of good comes from a little bit of good," or, in other words, where the positive social returns vastly exceed the amount of time and money invested. JEFF SKOLL

> *Recently retired, Michael had the time to review the annual report for his favourite cause. He used the Internet to do some more research and found out that the number of young abusers in his area had in fact been rising consistently for the past three years. He was shocked to learn that, despite his donations and those of many others, his organization had not been successful in addressing the problem of drug abuse among teens in his community. The programs the organization had in place weren't working. Why hadn't this been reported to him before? He wants to be proactive. What can he do now to help solve this problem?*

THE ISSUES

As we discussed in the introduction, as Canadians we want to be more involved in making sure that our donations are achieving their intended impact and doing as much good as they possibly can. But what do we mean by impact and how do we measure it?

Like in any contractual arrangement, your charity will agree to produce certain results in return for receiving your grant. You will provide them with funding in good faith and expect that they are able to achieve results. But things can go wrong in any organization. They may be a large administration struggling with bureaucracy and administrative costs, or they may face an unanticipated problem during the period after you provided a grant. You will want to make sure that your charity is doing what you have agreed to, achieving the expected results and meeting the agreed targets.

THE SOLUTIONS

Monitoring and Tracking Progress

You can get information on results from site visits, the charity's written reports, and from conversations with charity staff, board members and other philanthropists. To ensure the charity is achieving its deliverables, it is a good idea to take an analytical approach to your charity evaluation, just like you would evaluate a business for an investment. You need to understand your cause, the charities that support it and the environment in which they operate. The impact or results you want should already be clearly outlined in your strategic plan. Using this as your starting point, you can begin to monitor and track the performance of your grants and then ultimately evaluate your impact.

In tracking progress, you will want to measure the specific criteria you identified when selecting your charity, as outlined in Chapter 4. Have they made progress toward solving the problem they identified? Is the executive director managing the finances appropriately and keeping administrative costs down?

Evaluating Your Impact

Evaluation of your impact can involve information from many sources, and it can be time-consuming and expensive. However, collecting this information can give you the evidence you will need to understand whether your donation has made a real difference. A model for information tracking should be set up in advance with input and output data on specific indicators which point to the evidence that the program is achieving meaningful results. For example:

- What number of people have they helped through their specific program?
- What are the results on those individuals?
- Were individuals' problems solved on a permanent basis?
- Are there other services in the area which link to this program?
- What other indicators are there which might reinforce their results? (e.g. regional statistics for your specified cause).

Had Michael taken the time to understand this and review his organization regularly, he wouldn't have been so surprised by his recent research. If information had been collected on the wider context of teen drug abuse from the beginning of his charity's program, then short and longer term outcomes could have been monitored regularly for their impact.

In their book *Money Well Spent*, Paul Brest and Hal Harvey point out the distinction to be made between achieving an intended outcome and achieving an impact. Impact assumes causation—that the outcome would not have occurred without the stated intervention. A control group will help you understand what factors were beyond the program's control and how they may have affected the results. By putting a control group in place at the outset you can then collect data on your program from those people who experience the intervention and those who do not. Only then will you be able to obtain evidence that your intervention caused the outcome. You will be able to see if there is a statistically significant change in the group which received the intervention after accounting for other factors with the evidence from the control group.[1]

---

[1] Brest, Paul and Harvey, Hal. *Money Well Spent: A Strategic Plan for Smart Philanthropy*. 2008.

But this level of study can be difficult to come by. The alternative is to document observations about the group or a cross-section of it both before and after the intervention. It does not control well for other factors influencing change, but it can still be very useful and help to correlate the program's intervention with the outcome. "Anecdotal evidence, visits to services and the (success) stories of users will remain powerful influences on giving. It isn't uncommon to have no published evidence of impact; however, this does not mean a particular type of service or intervention is necessarily ineffective. This is a particularly important point for philanthropic giving, which often seeks to support and incubate new and innovative work, which by its very nature will not have an established evidence base."[2]

---

[2]McCarthy, Kerry. *Charity Impact Evaluation.* Matrix Knowledge Group. 2007.

IN SUMMARY

There can be tremendous benefits to monitoring and evaluating your gifts. You can assess your impact, charities can learn and use positive evidence to support future efforts, and end users can be assured that these services have a real benefit to their community or a working solution to their problem. However, there are also limitations of evaluation.

Evaluation can be hard to do in some cases and even observational evaluations can be expensive depending on where the program is operating. As a result, it may be very difficult to determine the effectiveness of programs. As Michael learned, evaluation can also be viewed as a way to identify failure, instead of a way to learn how to improve. Bad results are often not published or communicated widely. But by embracing evaluation and building a library of evidence in collaboration with donors, charities have the opportunity to streamline their efforts and become even more effective.

SUCCESS STORY

Cheryl and Rob McEwen began their philanthropy in 2003 after two deaths in their family, both due to cancer, caused them to reflect on what they could do to help. According to Cheryl, "Dealing with the hospitals and the treatment for our relatives was a real eye-opener. We saw the stress on our hospitals while we were there with our loved ones. We wondered how they would ever be able to cope with the baby boom generation entering the doors. We were aware that almost half of the Ontario budget goes to health care and wanted to do something that would help bring new treatments, reduce hospital stays and ultimately bring down some of the costs associated with health care. We already had a relationship with the Toronto General and Western Hospitals and we met with them to find out what we could do. They told us about the four platforms for the strategic plan for the hospitals and one of them, 'Regenerative Medicine', was clearly the most transformational. We met with key researchers in the field and learned about the potential for the body to repair itself through regenerative therapies and stem cell research. In 2003 very few people knew much about this field. We learned about the strength of scientific talent in Toronto moving into this area of research and how a gift from us could accelerate this research.

"We became very excited that regenerative medicine was the right cause. But we also realized that to make a real impact, we needed to focus on two key things: collaboration and strategic funding.

"In order to foster the collaboration between the great talent that was already in Toronto, we knew we needed to find the best stem cell scientist to run the McEwen Centre. We needed a world recognized leader to pull these great minds together in a collaborative format. So we developed an advisory board of internationally renowned scientists to help us develop a strategic plan and to recruit Dr. Gordon Keller from New York City's Mount Sinai Hospital. Fifteen top researchers from five hospitals in Toronto were chosen to join the McEwen Centre. Through all of this we had moved from being philanthropists to active philanthropy."

The McEwen Centre for Regenerative Medicine was established at University Health Network in 2003 with a generous $10 million donation from Rob and Cheryl McEwen, which they matched in 2006 with a second donation. The McEwen Centre's vision is to be a world-renowned centre for stem cell biology and regenerative medicine. To achieve this ambitious goal, the team of McEwen Investigators is working together to accelerate the development of more effective treatments for conditions such as heart disease, diabetes, respiratory disease and spinal cord injury. The McEwen Centre is based in the heart of Toronto's Discovery District at the MaRS Centre/Toronto Medical Discovery Tower.

Cheryl explained that, "Along with offering funding to these top scientists we felt that commercialization was another key to success. We wanted to provide seed funding to support research projects of great merit, assessing the risks. If we could commercialize this research we could change the model to help the centre ultimately become self-funding.

"Monitoring and evaluating our doctors' results is critical to our ongoing success. We hold quarterly meetings with Dr. Keller and review the doctor's research results. We also hold an annual McEwen retreat where all the doctors and researchers come together to present to one another. By sharing both their accomplishments and their unexpected findings the team establishes a great synergy and sharing of information. The old mindsets of protecting information are removed because the researchers feed off each other's presentations. Scientists want to advance their research and they get really excited when they learn how their colleagues have solved a problem or suggested a different approach. These group discussions are incredibly stimulating and productive.

"We are still in the early days of this research, but our results speak for themselves. Our researchers are learning to harness the power of stem cells to repair, regenerate or replace diseased cells, tissues and organs. We are working toward the reversal of the devastating effects of cardiovascular disease, allowing children with diabetes to live day to day without insulin injections or pumps. Far from a science fiction scenario, these are realistic goals. The tremendous therapeutic potential of stem cells lies in their remarkable ability to generate a variety of specialized cell types that could provide a renewable and virtually unlimited source of cells for cellular therapy and tissue engineering to treat diseases such as cancer, Parkinson's disease, Alzheimer's disease, spinal cord injury, heart disease, diabetes or osteoarthritis.

"My advice to anyone contemplating a large gift who wants to ensure they are effective is: Decide the area you want to be involved in, learn how your money will be spent and don't be shy about asking questions. Once you make your choice, set up the parameters for how your funds will be used and meet regularly with your charity to review progress.

"Our work in philanthropy has been extremely rewarding. We have had the opportunity to meet brilliant and committed people who are working on behalf of all of us for the betterment of our health. It has really broadened our perspective and we are truly honoured to be in a position to help these extremely driven scientists."

THINGS YOU NEED TO KNOW

- Evaluating the impact of your gift will help you understand how your gift has made a difference.
- Evaluation can be expensive and time-consuming.
- Establishing a control group is the best way to evaluate your impact.

QUESTIONS YOU NEED TO ASK

- What social return did you achieve with your investment?
- What method of evaluation will be best for your type of intervention?
- Did you find the right drivers for change?
- How can you ensure your resources achieve the greatest possible impact?
- Did your plan understand the social, political and economic factors that shape your cause?

THINGS YOU NEED TO DO

- Examine whether you achieved the results you set out to accomplish.
- Meet regularly with your charity to review progress.

DECISIONS YOU NEED TO MAKE

- Decide whether you want to fund general operating expenses or, if you prefer, how you can ensure all of your money goes directly to the program and not to general administration.

MASTER YOUR PHILANTHROPY
Monitor and Evaluate Your Impact

TIPS

- Use your strategic plan as a starting point of reference for evaluation.
- Ask all the questions you can and don't be afraid to sound silly.

TRAPS

- Likewise, don't be afraid of evaluation. We won't learn anything if we hide our mistakes. Be open and share your learning with others.

Principle Mastery: Impact assumes causation–that the outcome would not have occurred without the stated intervention. Establishing measurement criteria including a control group in advance of the program's start will help you understand what factors were beyond the program's control and how they affected the results.

CHAPTER 9

Succession Planning for Your Philanthropy

No matter what you've done for yourself or for humanity, if you can't look back on having given love and attention to your own family, what have you really accomplished? LEE IACOCCA

> Gary was 55 and financially secure. He had inherited control of his father's successful business and he was president of their considerable family foundation. He comes from a large family and many of his siblings were shareholders but not working in the business. Although the family spent little time together, demands for increased payouts from the business were common and there was little support for any further funding of the foundation. What is more, Gary had no plan for transferring either the business or the leadership for the foundation. The problem was, his family couldn't agree on their goals. There was distrust among his brothers and sisters and they lacked the skills to communicate with and listen to each other. Gary tried to bring in outside directors to help, but this had been met with skepticism by the family.
>
> Although Dad had been successful in business, both his parents were consumed by it and had spent little time at home when their children were young. Gary was determined to make his family legacy a meaningful one and he wanted to ensure that his own children didn't find themselves in a similar situation. But with all the sibling rivalry, how was Gary going to ensure that his family's legacy lived on?

THE ISSUES

Distributing the wealth you have is a big and important job, and it can be extremely stressful. Bill Gates is doing that now, so that his children won't have to. How do you teach the value of stewardship and the importance of giving back? In retrospect, what might Gary's parents have done to avoid the situation he is facing now?

THE SOLUTIONS

There are a number of important things to consider when you are setting the wheels in motion to implement your succession plan and giving strategy.

- **Identify the successors** for your wealth and for your philanthropy and ensure that they understand their responsibilities.
- **Focus on your current life stage** and that of your successors to determine what kind of gifts might be appropriate for you.
- **Mobilize your advisors** to ensure that your overall wealth management plan includes both a succession plan for the transition of your wealth and your charitable intentions.

Identifying the successors

Many families struggle with the question of how to instill desired family values in their children and ensure that they are motivated to achieve, even if they will inherit significant wealth. In fact, the biggest worry reported by high-net-worth individuals is their ability to maintain a work ethic and sense of values in the family.[1] Without this sense of values and responsibility, many children of the wealthy suffer from 'affluenza'—lack of ambition or aspiration brought on by a life of wealth and privilege. Even families without wealth can experience this if important values are not instilled at an early age.

There are a number of lessons to be learned from long-lasting successful families in business that can be applied here through a lens of philanthropy.

---

[1] Stenner Investment Partners, *Truewealth Report*, Sensus Research Inc., 2006. www.truewealthreport.com

John. L. Ward points to many of these in his book, *Perpetuating the Family Business*, and some of these lessons are summarized below.[2] They include respecting the challenge of transitioning your wealth, and the importance of perspective, communication, parenting and planning. Let's examine some of these now.

Respect the challenge

If you want to pass a legacy on to your children and beyond, you must consider planning now for your succession. Larger and more complex philanthropic strategies require more sophisticated managers of wealth, so education on the responsibilities of stewardship is important. As discussed in Chapter 3, one of the keys to ensuring success is to develop your vision/mission together with your family, partners and your advisors too.

Having a values-based discussion now and identifying the things most important to you can help to ensure agreement and acknowledgement of the responsibilities of stewardship. Even if your family is spread out with grandparents moving away to a tax haven and siblings and offspring all over the country, making the effort to get their input and involving them in the planning process will help to foster commitment and get family members to take responsibility for the honour of philanthropy.

Another way to help ensure your children will respect the challenge is to establish and maintain a work ethic. This requires that they have direct experience doing work. Whatever the job is, encouraging children to work will help instill a sense of respect for what they have and provide a source of satisfaction or pride in their achievement.

Family involvement in your charitable activities can also engage your children and give them direct experience with charitable organizations and the joy of successfully helping others. Alternatively, a position on the board of a family foundation or directing a donor-advised fund can help to instill the value of money and of stewardship. Aligning family values by involving and consulting your successors early is the best way to ensure your legacy and wishes are not challenged from the grave. Families that

---

[2] Ward, John. L. *Perpetuating the Family Business*, Palgrave MacMillan, 2004.

respect this challenge have a better chance of success in carrying on the family legacy, fostering family unity and encouraging commitment.

Perspectives on the same issue will be different
Another lesson from successful families is to gain the perspective of others. Many families have benefited from outside help in their business or on the board of their foundations. Alternative perspectives help us to see an issue from all sides. Success can be achieved by respecting those views and rising above diverging attitudes.

Gary himself sees the value in gaining outside perspectives, but without the channels of communication being open, he has not been able to convince his siblings to give it a try.

Communication is indispensable
Communication is critical in everything we do in life but it is sometimes a difficult thing to achieve, especially in family dynamics. Successful families have used formalized family member meetings to open up communication. These meetings can be facilitated by someone outside if required, but educating your family in the skills of communication, empathy, listening and compromise will be the key to a successful transition of leadership for your philanthropy. At the end of the day, it is our actions that set the example.

Parenting
There is no substitute for your time and open regular dialogue about the values you hold most dear to teach your children about the responsibility of money. Many parents fail to do this, but those who are committed to being actively involved in the lives of their children and grandchildren, talking about the issues that are important to them as part of their daily routine, have successfully instilled important values into their children and helped to teach them valuable life lessons. For example, rewarding children for reaching goals helps them to understand what expectations they must meet to succeed. This will help them to focus on building competencies and to feel pride in earning the privileges awarded them. It will also help them to assess where their philanthropy should be focused as they evaluate organizations that support their cause.

Another example is treating wealth with balance—it is neither denied nor flaunted. Being understated helps children learn not to be focused on consuming wealth ostentatiously. Children reared with this in mind tend not to see wealth itself as the goal, but as a means to achieve broader goals. This can be translated into applying those goals into their community and their chosen causes.

Life Stages

As you move through life, your lifestyle and financial circumstances change—and so do the ways you might choose to support your favourite cause. How can you determine what kind of gifts are a good fit for you based on your current life stage?

Encouraging your young family members whose means may be limited to budget for making small cash donations and to actively participate in charity events can be good ways to kick-start a lifetime of philanthropy. And as they start to earn money of their own, monthly paycheque giving or pre-authorized withdrawals by credit card are easy and effective ways to build a commitment to philanthropy in the early years.

Our 40's and 50's are often peak earnings years and can also be when personal debt is at its highest. During these middle age years, people are busy and philanthropy can often be far from top of mind. But this is a time when there is also a great need for tax savings and as outlined in Chapter 2, there are many ways to give now. By donating your existing life policy and making the charity owner and beneficiary of the policy, you are eligible for a donation receipt for the cash value of the policy and each future premium paid. You can use these receipts to claim a tax credit on your return. And for those who hold publicly traded securities which have appreciated in value, or stock options, donating these securities can give you immediate tax relief by eliminating all or some of your capital gains tax payable.

Generally, people make planned gifts as they approach retirement, when they are preparing their wills or establishing an estate plan, or when significant events (like a death, divorce, the sale of a major asset) force a change in their life's circumstances. If you are retired and looking for a dependable income stream, gifts combined with annuities can be used to meet your income needs in a tax-efficient manner while ensuring a gift for your cause. At this stage, many people will allow for their charitable gifts by making specific bequests in their will. And designating charities as beneficiaries of the proceeds from RRSPs or RRIFs or life insurance policies can ensure a sizeable gift while reducing taxes payable by your estate.

Even if you have done a good job instilling your family values and teaching your children about stewardship of money and the responsibilities of wealth, things happen. This is why it is important to keep your wealth plan up to date, especially if the successors you have identified end up being irresponsible or unable to manage as you had intended. Major business, personal and financial decision events happen throughout our lives and they represent one of greatest opportunities to seek help from astute advisors.

Mobilize Your Advisors

Your financial advisors will be particularly interested in discussing your plans and the vision/mission of your philanthropy. They can directly help you and your family keep your focus on your mission, vision, values, goals and personal preferences, and they can introduce various structures, strategies and financial tools to execute your plan. But how do you teach your children or heirs to know the difference between good and bad advice? For that matter, how can you determine the difference?

Look for an advisor who seems to really care about you and your family and is non-judgmental towards any poor decisions you may have made. Good advisors have a keen appreciation for the emotional and psychological aspects of money and how we deal with it, which is critical to our success in managing our money. Their advice should be practical, easy to understand and down-to-earth, and cut through all the confusing, contradictory information you hear and read. They should explain the reasoning behind their advice and empower you to learn to make your own financial decisions wisely.[3]

---

[3]Vohwinkle, Jeremy. *About.com Guide to Financial Planning*.

Planning is Essential

Long-lasting, successful family businesses plan strategically for their future and review their plans regularly. Your advisor should be able to help you with this, but as highlighted earlier in this book, your vision for strategic giving is more likely to succeed if you have a defined process in place, starting with a strategic direction or mission statement, and some specific objectives that govern both your giving and an action plan. In addition to this, putting a plan in place to ensure the successful transition of your family's philanthropy and its continuity once you are gone is important. Your advisor should be able to help you incorporate your philanthropic goals into your overall wealth management plan and will review that plan with you annually.

IN SUMMARY

You have an obligation when you have money to put it to good use. What better way to teach your children about the value of giving back? The lessons learned from other successful families can be a good guide and can help to ensure success in carrying on the family legacy, fostering family unity and encouraging commitment in your successors.

SUCCESS STORY

Thane Stenner is the founder of Stenner Investment Partners and a partner and managing director at GMP Private Client in Vancouver. Thane's practice limits its client list to a core group of individuals and families with net assets of $10 million or more. Within this framework, his team can take the significant time required to build the deep, one-on-one relationships required to truly understand their client families. Their goal is to help clients to create successful wealth plans that preserve, and continue to enhance, their families' lifestyles and legacies—and that includes philanthropy and gift planning.

Confidential research into Thane's client base and their peers revealed that less than 1% of these successful people chose philanthropy as a primary driver of family values, but that isn't really surprising, according to Thane.

"The ultra-wealthy are just not wired to think about philanthropy first, particularly while they are building their wealth. Once they have satisfied their lifestyle considerations however, they become more philanthropic and devote more time to their favourite causes. So, although philanthropy isn't their primary driver, almost 70% donated over $100,000 in the previous year and 60% of them ranked one of the top 3 reasons to give as 'strategic personal tax and estate benefits.' My clients tend to have a generosity of spirit; they are generous with staff and with extended family members. Those with the highest evolution of that spirit tend to have had parents and grandparents that imbued it.

"We all have obligations as citizens to educate our youth about the value of philanthropy and helping others less fortunate than ourselves. One of my most successful clients, in terms of philanthropy, comes from an iconic west-coast family in business. His parents felt that living up to being a good steward of their wealth was an important trait. They had regular discussions around the dinner table about helping people—who they were helping and why they were doing so. This family has evolved to a state where they have a family mission statement for their business and for their own private foundation. They hold regular meetings to dialogue on where to collectively give in order to create a larger impact.

"Parents who have simply provided money to their children tend to be the ones who have had the most trouble. 'Affluenza' can manifest itself in many ways in children, from low motivation levels to lack of drive to educate themselves and, in the extreme cases, to drugs and alcohol abuse. This is why it is especially important for the children of the wealthy to have a sense of responsibility, not just to steward their own wealth but also to give back by helping their families and their communities. Those who truly take the time to be with their kids and teach them these responsibilities are far more likely to succeed in instilling balance.

"The most important thing is that it comes from the heart. Philanthropy cannot be a forced ideology of what is worthy. My successful clients haven't handcuffed their kids with their own causes, but encouraged their children to become involved and donate to things that they are passionate about. And our clients who give are often blessed in ways that are unexpected. Even those who shun recognition for their gifts experience the joy that only true generosity can bring, especially when they see their kids taking up whatever their chosen cause is."

THINGS YOU NEED TO KNOW

- The biggest worry reported by high-net-worth individuals is their ability to maintain a work ethic and sense of values in their family.
- Successful families respect the challenge of being good stewards of their wealth.

QUESTIONS YOU NEED TO ASK

- Is my family communicating openly and regularly about the values important to us?
- Am I spending enough time talking to my family about the issues that are important to me and them?
- Am I teaching my children the skills of empathy, listening and compromise that will help them to understand different perspectives on the same issue?

THINGS YOU NEED TO DO

- Identify the successors for your wealth and for your philanthropy and ensure that they understand their responsibilities.
- Focus on your current life stage and that of your successors to determine what kind of gifts might be appropriate for you.
- Mobilize your advisors to ensure that your overall wealth management plan includes both a succession plan for the transition of your wealth and your charitable intentions.

DECISIONS YOU NEED TO MAKE

- If communication, succession planning or transition is a problem, consider bringing in an outside advisor to assist.

MASTER YOUR PHILANTHROPY
Succession Planning for Your Philanthropy

TIPS

- One way to help ensure your children will respect and steward their wealth appropriately is to establish and maintain a work ethic early on.
- Try to open up lines of communication by setting up a regular family meeting.

TRAPS

- Don't let your work consume you. There is no substitute for your time and open regular dialogue with your family about the values you hold most dear.

Principle Mastery: Families that respect the challenge of being good stewards of their wealth have a better chance of success in perpetuating the family legacy.

Conclusion

Canada is a wealthy nation and as Canadians we are blessed in many ways. But the disparity between rich and poor in our society and around the world continues to widen. If we see our personal wealth not only as a means to live well, but as a way to contribute, then we will become part of the solution. Whatever stage you are in, or whatever amount of money or time you might be able to contribute, your chances for success are greatly enhanced if you develop a plan and take the long-term view.

Besides making you a part of the solution, philanthropy will make you happier! You have heard from real philanthropists about the joy they experience in their giving. Their money doesn't necessarily buy happiness, but philanthropy does. The emotional return they get on their investment, although difficult to quantify, is certainly higher. In his book *Gross National Happiness*, Arthur C. Brookes explores 'the pursuit of happiness' in America and what makes people happy. It is interesting because it is more than anecdotal. His findings are backed by considerable scientific research. "The data prove this point overwhelmingly... people who give money to charity are... more likely than non-givers to say they are very happy.... and the more people give, the happier they get.... Giving delivers direct psychological and physiological benefits."[1]

---

[1] Brooks, Arthur C. *Gross National Happiness*, Basic Books, 2008.

Planning your gifts as a part of your overall wealth management plan is just the smart thing to do. There are many ways to increase the size of your gifts and reduce your taxes payable by taking advantage of the tax incentives we have in Canada. Take advantage of those incentives and speak with your financial advisors about your charitable intentions. They can help you to find the right solutions for your circumstances.

I hope that in reading the chapters of this book that you have been able to reflect on your own philanthropy, identify with some of the issues and problems raised and that you have found some guidance in the solutions presented. The instructions offered here are not my instructions. They are lessons that reflect what real philanthropists and advisors have learned about how to make an effective impact for the causes closest to heart. Even if you only take some of the elements covered here, or you address them in your own way, the important thing is that you start to think strategically about mastering your philanthropy.

Finally, I would like to express my sincere appreciation to the many people who have helped, coached, edited and allowed themselves to be interviewed for this book. I will be forever grateful.

NICOLA ELKINS

Gift Planning Matrix

Type of Gift	Benefits to the Donor	Acceptable Assets	Most Appropriate For
Outright Gift of Cash	• Donation receipt for full amount • Straightforward transactions • Satisfaction of seeing gift at work today	• Cash • Cheque • Credit Card • Pre-Authorized Contributions (PAC), usually paid monthly	• Everyone (any age) who can afford to give up some principal and the interest it would otherwise earn
A Gift of Publicly Listed securities (including segregated & mutual fund units)	• Donation receipt for fair market value • No capital gains tax • Satisfaction of seeing gift at work today	• Stocks • Bonds • Mutual Fund Units • Employee Stock Option Shares	• Owners (any age) of stocks, bonds and other securities who can afford to give the asset and the interest or dividends it earns
Life Insurance Policy (Charity named as owner and irrevocable beneficiary)	• Donation receipt for cash value and any future premiums paid • Small current outlay leveraged into larger future gift	• Any whole life policy (participating or universal) • Term policy (personal)	• Persons (generally ages 30-60) who i) have an older policy no longer needed, or ii) want to make a large gift but have limited resources
Life Insurance (Charity named as beneficiary but not owner)	• Satisfaction of providing a future gift while retaining full control of policy • Donation receipt to estate for full value of death proceeds	• Any type of life insurance policy	• Persons (any age) whose personal needs and family situation may be subject to change
Bequest of Retirement Plan Accumulations	• Satisfaction of providing a possible future gift while preserving personal security • Gift receipt that offsets tax on distribution of retirement funds	• Registered Retirement Savings Plan (RRSP) and Registered Retirement Income Fund (RRIF) accumulations	• All individuals, but especially single persons, and surviving spouses who have made other provisions for heirs

Type of Gift	Benefits to the Donor	Acceptable Assets	Most Appropriate For
Bequest by Will	• Satisfaction of providing for future gift while retaining full control of property • Donation receipt for use with final income tax return • For bequest of listed securities, no capital gain tax, for most other property 50% of capital gain will be taxable but can be offset by tax credit from gift, likely resulting in tax savings to estate.	• Cash, securities, real estate, tangible personal property	• All individuals (any age), but especially older persons with few or no heirs
Shares in a privately-owned corporation	• Public charity – Donation receipt for appraised market value at time of gift, issued immediately (if gift to public charity) • Private Foundation – Donation receipt issued only when foundation sells shares. Receipt value is the lesser of amount realized by foundation and the fair market value at time of gift. • **50%** of capital gain taxable, offset by tax credit from donation receipt	• Shares held in privately-owned corporation	• Entrepreneurs who are philanthropic • Venture philanthropists

Type of Gift	Benefits to the Donor	Acceptable Assets	Most Appropriate For
Outright Gift of Real Estate	• Donation receipt for fair market value (FMV) determined by appraisal (independently obtained by charity) • **50%** of gain taxable (unless property is donor's primary residence, in which case no taxable capital gain), offset by tax credit from donation receipt	• Real Estate	• Owners (generally over 50) of a principal residence or investment property who do not need the property or the proceeds from its sale
Outright "In-Kind" Gift of Tangible Personal Property (other than cultural property)	• Donation receipt (if applicable) for fair market value determined by appraisal • **50%** of gain taxable, offset by tax credit from donation • Satisfaction of seeing gift at work now or in near term	• Artworks, furniture, equipment, collections, automobiles, musical instruments	• Owners (generally over age 50) of objects which they no longer intend to use
Charitable Remainder Trust (CRT)	• Net income from property for life or a term of years • Donation receipt issued for present value of the remainder interest - issued at time trust established • Property not subject to probate	• Cash, securities, real estate	• Persons (generally over age 60) who want to make a future gift and obtain present tax relief but want to preserve investment income for themselves and/or a survivor
Gift of Residual Interest in real estate or artworks	• Ability to continue using property for life or term of years • Donation receipt for present value of residual interest issued at time of gift • Avoidance of tax of a portion of capital gain if donor retains life interest • Property not subject to probate	• Principal residence, other real estate, artworks	• Persons (generally over age 60) who otherwise would give the property under their will

Type of Gift	Benefits to the Donor	Acceptable Assets	Most Appropriate For
Outright Gift of Certified Cultural Property	• Donation receipt for fair market value determined by appraisal • **100%** contribution limit • No tax on capital gain • Satisfaction of preserving property of national significance	• Artworks, collections, artifacts or historic structures certified by Cultural Property Review Board (CPRB)	• Owners (generally over age 50) of cultural treasures who would like to preserve the property within Canada
Interest-free Loan (normally payable on demand)	• Principal is recoverable • Interest earned on loaned funds not taxable to donor • Satisfaction of helping charity today	• Cash and cash equivalents	• Persons (any age) who have more than enough current income but want to preserve all principal for their own future security and/or heirs
Charitable Gift Annuity (self-insured)[1]	• Guaranteed life payments, all or substantially tax-free • A donation receipt for a portion of contribution	• Cash or marketable securities	• Oldest donors (usually 65 and older) who want the security of guaranteed income payments
Charitable Gift Annuity (reinsured)[2]		• Cash or marketable securities	• Oldest donors (usually 65 and older) who want the security of guaranteed income payments

1 **Note:** Only charities designated as charitable organizations (i.e. not public or private foundations) and authorized under provincial law, may currently issue gift annuities.
2 **Note:** Currently public and private foundations, including Canada's Community Foundations, may not reinsure gift annuities.

Source: Professional Advisors eResource. Community Foundations of Canada. Adapted and revised from Minton & Somers, *Planned Giving for Canadians*, 2006.

Index

A

annuity, annuities 23, 29, 33, 104, 116
assets 8, 21, 23, 28, 32, 75, 79-80, 82, 87, 106, 113-116

B

beneficiaries 21, 26-27, 34, 39, 104
beneficiary 23, 26, 28, 103, 113
bequest 23, 26, 28, 104, 113-114

C

Canada Revenue Agency (CRA) 12, 32, 51, 62, 79-81, 87, 90
Canadian Association of Gift Planners 16, 31
Canadian Cultural Property Export Review Board 24
capital dividend accounts 28
capital gains tax 8, 14, 24, 29, 103, 113
capital property 23
cash gift 23
certified cultural property 24, 116
charitable sector 11-18, 85
charitable status 12, 14, 87

D

death benefits 27
deferred gift 26
disbursement quota 79, 82
donation limit 23, 33
donor-advised fund 15, 25, 60, 62, 67, 101

E

eco-gifts 24
endowment 15, 25, 60, 62, 67, 82
estate plan 20, 21, 103
evaluating 8, 52, 91, 93, 95-96
executor 21

F

fiduciary 31, 80-82, 87
flow-through limited partnership 27
foundation 13-15, 25, 60, 79-88, 99, 101-102, 114, 116
  community foundation 15, 31, 116
  private foundation 14, 37, 45, 60-62, 67-68, 81-82, 87, 107, 114, 116
  public foundation 15, 43, 60, 81, 87
fundraising 8, 51, 86

G

gift planning 9, 16, 18, 19-35, 106, 113-116
gift matching 24, 73
governance 38, 80-85
grant proposal 50, 51, 53, 55

I

in-kind 8, 35, 115
insured share bequest 28

L

legacy 7-8, 25, 26, 33, 37, 43, 99, 101, 102, 106, 109
liability 24, 80
life insurance 23, 25, 27-29, 104, 113

M

microfinancing 64
mission statement 38-39, 42, 85, 105, 107

N

not-for-profit (NFP) 12-13, 42, 59, 80

P

power of attorney 21, 34
property transfer 21, 33

R

receipt 23-27, 29, 35, 62, 79, 103, 113-116
registered charity 14, 23, 82
RRIF 26, 28-29, 33, 104, 113
RRSP 23, 26, 28, 104, 113

S

securities 8, 14, 23-24, 27-28, 33, 35, 74, 103, 113-116
social entrepreneurship 28, 63
socially responsible investment 64
stock options 20, 24, 29, 33, 103
strategic philanthropy 7, 43
strategic plan 7, 17, 38-48, 50, 56, 65, 72, 85, 90, 93-94, 97

T

tax credit 8, 14, 22-23, 27-29, 33, 35, 73, 103, 114-115
tax deduction 22, 29
tax incentives 17, 112
tax planning 21, 33
taxable income 22, 74
triple-bottom-line accounting 70
trust 62, 74, 80-82, 115

V

venture philanthropy 63
vision 7, 9, 26, 38-40, 54, 75, 94, 101, 104-105

W

wealth replacement 28

Other Titles in The Knowledge Bureau's Master Your Series